8 KEYS TO
END
EMOTIONAL
EATING

8 Keys to Mental Health Series
Babette Rothschild, Series Editor

The 8 Keys series of books provides readers with brief, inexpensive, and high-quality self-help books on a variety of topics in mental health. Each volume is written by an expert in the field, someone who is capable of presenting evidence-based information in a concise and clear way. These books stand out by offering consumers cutting-edge, relevant theory in easily digestible portions, written in an accessible style. The tone is respectful of the reader and the messages are immediately applicable. Filled with exercises and practical strategies, these books empower readers to help themselves.

8 KEYS TO END EMOTIONAL EATING

HOWARD S. FARKAS

W. W. NORTON & COMPANY
Independent Publishers Since 1923

8 Keys to End Emotional Eating is intended as a general information resource; it is not a substitute medical or psychological treatment and may not be relied upon for purposes of diagnosing or treating any illness. Please seek out professional care from a licensed clinician if you are pregnant, nursing or experiencing symptoms of any potentially serious condition. Individuals and case examples described in this book are composite portraits representing no particular persons, living or dead, and any resemblance of names or descriptions to actual persons is coincidental.

For information about permission to reproduce selections from this book, write to Permissions, W. W. Norton & Company, Inc., 500 Fifth Avenue, New York, NY 10110

For information about special discounts for bulk purchases, please contact W. W. Norton Special Sales at specialsales@wwnorton.com or 800-233-4830

Manufacturing by Sheridan Books
Production manager: Katelyn MacKenzie

Library of Congress Cataloging-in-Publication Data

Names: Farkas, Howard (Howard S.)
Title: 8 keys to end emotional eating / Howard Farkas.
Other titles: Eight keys to emotional eating
Description: First edition. | New York : W.W. Norton & Company, [2019] |
    Series: 8 keys to mental health series | Includes bibliographical
    references and index.
Identifiers: LCCN 2019015768 | ISBN 9780393712322 (pbk.)
Subjects: LCSH: Compulsive eating—Popular works. | Compulsive
    eating—Prevention. | Food habits—Psychological aspects.
Classification: LCC RC552.C65 F37 2019 | DDC 616.85/26—dc23
LC record available at https://lccn.loc.gov/2019015768

W. W. Norton & Company, Inc., 500 Fifth Avenue, New York, N.Y. 10110
www.wwnorton.com

W. W. Norton & Company Ltd., 15 Carlisle Street, London W1D 3BS

1 2 3 4 5 6 7 8 9 0

To Debi, for providing the balance that made this possible

Contents

Foreword

Babette Rothschild, Series Editor, 8 Keys to Mental Health
author of *The Body Remembers*, Volumes 1 & 2

Emotions usually go hand-in-hand with eating. Our feelings primarily dictate when, what, and with whom we eat. We eat to celebrate, to console, to get energized, to relax, to remember, to commune. We eat when we are anxious or sad, and we eat when we are happy and joyous. Who has not eaten, at times, to curb sexual frustration or enjoy an after-glow? The pairing of emotions with eating is normal and most of the time is not problematic. However, when normal eating behaviors mutate into emotional eating, that is, uncontrolled and unwanted eating, that is problematic. In this volume, *8 Keys to End Emotional Eating*, Dr. Howard Farkas sheds a much-needed a spotlight on the types of emotional eating that are highly dysfunctional, leading to low self-image, weight gain, obesity, and ill physical and mental health.

Wherever you live and whatever your culture, you and I probably share a lot of similar experiences with dieting, weight loss, and diet books. Speaking for myself, over my—now fairly long—life (nearly 70! at this writing), I have probably read the majority of books on nutrition and weight loss, and I have tried most of the popular diets—Weight Watchers, Atkins (now renamed Ketogenic), The Zone, South Beach, Intermittent Fasting, and so on. Over the years I have had degrees of lesser and greater success.

Looking back, I can see that my relationship to food and eating, to myself, as well as body image, has gradually changed for the better. These days I rarely (less than once a month) overeat and never binge. Like most of my friends and colleagues, I have become much more conscious and conscientious about healthy food choices and portions. I eat fewer sweets than I used to, though I do make sure to have some dark chocolate everyday— thank goodness for those studies that proved it is healthy! That said, with regard to weight and diet, I consider myself to continue to be a "work in progress."

As I was reading this volume, I was reminded of the book that greatly impacted my relationship to food back in the early 1980s. Originally published in 1978, Susie Orbach's *Fat is a Feminist Issue* was revolutionary for me. My life altering takeaway was her view on the effects of dieting deprivation and how that sabotages weight loss. Following Orbach's manifesto, I began keeping forbidden foods on hand in my home and allowing myself to eat them— guilt free! —whenever I wished. At first I was nervous to let myself loose in this way. But what I found out was this: when those foods I was used to craving were readily available, my longing for them gradually diminished. That is not to say that I lost interest in them altogether, but that I discovered that I indulged them significantly less frequently and in smaller amounts than I would have ever predicted. This change did not happen immediately, nonetheless, within a relatively short period of time I felt (and became) in control of my cravings. Since, I have continued to follow that same advice. Many of my friends gasp when they see that I keep multiple kinds of chocolate and other sweets, as well as temptations such as potato chips in my cupboards and fridge. And they are equally surprised to find out that I do not eat them all at once, all the time, or even everyday. It's a comfort for me to know those treats are there when I want them, not forbidden, so I find that I want them much, much less. This is actually the same philosophy used by the famous and much beloved See's Candies. The rule in their shops is that employees can eat as much of the chocolates as they want. No restrictions! Many times I have asked a sales person how they manage it. Invariably each has told me that initially they eat several candies a day, but that quickly it looses its allure. In fairly quick shift they pare down to one piece, or even none, per day. All would agree that giving employees free access to the chocolate is a very wise policy!

The reason I am telling these stories is because I was very happy to find that one of Farkas's central recommendations is similar. As he puts it: No food is forbidden. He writes, "There are no foods that you must avoid." and "Every thing is on the menu; the only question is: What do you want to eat?" I do not have an abstract understanding of this viewpoint. This is something that I have experienced and lived, for decades, so I have to agree. It saddens me when a friend tells me that they can not keep this or that beloved food in their home because they do not believe they can control their urges and cravings.

This is not a diet book. It is a life book. Throughout 8 *Keys to End Emotional Eating,* Farkas will help you to gain control over this aspect of your life that feels out of control. He is not going to tell you what to eat or how to diet. It is not a nutritional guide. Farkas is not going to talk to you about the usual emotions most people associate with overeating: sadness, anxiety, depression. Those topics already proliferate the libraries of people struggling with overeating and being overweight. And, unfortunately, for many readers, those books do not give them the help they hoped to find: to really, once and for all, conquer their relationship with food and maintain healthy eating and a healthy weight. Farkas has looked far further into the roots of overeating, down to the core: He will help you to change your relationship with food and with yourself.

Acknowledgments

I'm grateful to my editors at Norton, Deborah Malmud and Babette Rothschild, for considering this book to be a worthy addition to Norton's series, 8 Keys to Mental Health; and to Mariah Eppes and Sara McBride for their help in guiding me through the process. Their feedback and advice in helping to shape this book from beginning to end were invaluable. I'm also indebted to Candace Johnson whose editorial help on early drafts of this book helped transform it into a manuscript worthy of submitting.

My colleagues and friends at Northwestern Medicine's Wellness Institute, whose empathic approach to the treatment of obesity helped me to better understand the experience of our patients who struggled through the process of trying to lose weight. Special thanks to the medical director, Robert Kushner, for his encouragement when I first presented the central idea of the balance model at our weekly staff meeting. My appreciation for their influence on my thinking, of course, does not imply their endorsement of all the ideas in this book.

Kassie Brandenborg and Rebecca Leslie, former post-docs at Chicago Behavioral Health, and now valued colleagues, provided valuable feedback on earlier versions of the book, and shared their clinical experiences and insights about emotional eating while learning and applying the approach I describe. The doctoral students in Northwestern's clinical psychology program who participated over the years in my class on motivation and self-control helped me think through these ideas with their inquisitive and stimulating discussions. I'm also very indebted to many of my colleagues at Northwestern's clinical psychology program, particularly Mark Reinecke and Jason Washburn.

Several colleagues in social psychology whose research interests include motivation and the problem of self-control were very generous with their time and thoughts over the years. I'm especially grateful to Dan Molden and Eli Finkel at Northwestern, and Mickey Inzlicht at the University of Toronto, for spending time over drinks at conferences and lunches in Evanston discussing their research and offering helpful feedback about the ideas in this book.

I'm grateful to all of my wonderful friends and family members who were so supportive, especially those who took the time to read all or some of the early drafts and offered very helpful input. Special thanks to my daughter, Dafna Farkas, whose less-is-more editorial approach, and her familiarity with my tendency to over-explain, was extremely helpful in the final stages of editing.

Finally, I want to thank my patients, past and present, who shared their struggles with emotional eating, and provided the most invaluable insights to help me better understand this problem from their point of view. The stories that are presented as case examples throughout this book are composites of the narratives shared by all of the patients whom I've treated for this problem over the past 15 years. Any descriptions of individual details have been changed to protect their privacy while preserving the essence of the experiences that so many emotional eaters share.

8 KEYS TO
END
EMOTIONAL
EATING

INTRODUCTION

Megan

Megan's friends were taking her out to celebrate her engagement, and they chose her favorite place for dinner. She and her fiancée decided to get married in six months. Megan was determined to lose the weight she had gained over the past year, so she could walk down the aisle with confidence. She planned to begin a new diet the next day.

When she joined the others at the table, the server had just taken her friends' orders and asked Megan if she needed some more time to look at the menu.

"No thanks, I know exactly what I want," she replied.

She knew that the best item on the menu was the blackened redfish, grilled and seasoned just right, and she was looking forward to having it again. It was also one of the lower-calorie options available and would be a good way to restart her diet.

As the server turned to put in the orders, Megan saw someone at the next table get the three-cheese lasagna. She had tried it once before and thought it was nothing special, certainly not as good as the blackened redfish, and definitely not worth the extra calories. But now she decided that she wanted it anyway and asked the server to change her order.

The next morning, she went online to find a therapist who could help her with emotional eating and made an appointment to see me the following week.

Megan told me this story during our first session. Ever since she began dieting in high school, she had a pattern of starting a new diet that she would sabotage soon afterward by binge eating. She explained that these episodes had become more frequent over time, and she became increasingly anxious about how out of control she felt around food. She recognized that ordering the lasagna was just the latest episode in this long pattern, and now, as an adult, it was finally time for her to do something about it.

When she finished telling me about what happened at the restaurant and her history of dieting and emotional eating, I asked her what was on her mind when she decided to change her order. Her answer wasn't surprising because I had heard it many times before.

She said, "I just wanted to be bad."

The Mystery of Unwanted Eating

Megan's desire to be bad highlights an important aspect of the emotional eating experience, what I call the *transgressive motive*. It's a taboo-breaking thrill of defying the rules: "I don't care—I'm just gonna do it!"

I believe this motivation may be a factor underlying a variety of similarly unwanted behaviors, such as binge drinking, shopping splurges, and procrastination, among others. But the focus of this book is on the area that I specialize in: unwanted, compulsive eating. I'll explain how understanding emotional eating as an act of defiance can help end the behavior.

This is the problem that Megan asked me to help her with. She had a long pattern of losing weight and then regaining it, and she struggled with binge-like episodes while going through this up-and-down cycle. She recognized that eating anything from her long list of forbidden foods (pasta being just one example) was something she would have done in the past to sabotage any diet that she had begun. Her decision to change her order in the restaurant was just the latest incident that finally made undeniable to her what had been going on for years. The fact that she chose something that represented being bad—especially on the eve of beginning a new diet—illustrates a common and central characteristic of emotional eating.

If you struggle with emotional eating, then you've probably asked yourself, "Why am I doing this?" "I know exactly what I *should* do and what I want to do—so why can't I just stop?" or "How can I be in control of so much of my life, but not something as simple as eating?!" These are the types of questions that I hear often from my patients, especially when they first explain why they're coming in for help. In this book, I address these questions in the same way that I do in therapy: first by describing what emotional eating is and what drives it, then by explaining how you can stop it, and finally, how to adopt a more normal and enjoyable pattern of eating.

You've probably come up with your own list of reasons for why you eat when you don't want to. But collecting more explanations only distracts from focusing on the real cause and gets you further away from understanding the behavior. You won't find the answer among the usual suspects that most people assume to be the problem: weak willpower, poor self-control, temptation, stress relief, comfort, and so on. Instead, I offer a single explanation that will allow you to focus on understanding the underlying cause of emotional eating and stop the unwanted behavior for good.

That basic idea can be stated very briefly: *Unwanted eating is a defiant response to feeling controlled.* More specifically, the behavior is the result of an internal conflict between our need to feel accepted and our need for autonomy. Dieting reflects a basic human need for belonging. Making that sacrifice in a culture that stigmatizes

people who are overweight is seen as a way to feel worthy of acceptance. But eventually, dieting can provoke an exaggerated show of
autonomy to counterbalance the sacrifice.

This model provides a framework to put unwanted behavior in
a context that can help you make sense of it. The mechanism is
somewhat analogous to Newton's third law of motion: "For every
action there is an equal and opposite reaction." In terms of emotional eating, this means that after an accumulated buildup of
resentment about giving in to outside pressure (especially, but not
only, around dieting), there's an equal and opposite urge for defiant, unrestrained eating. The main practical implication of this
idea is that, paradoxically, it's easier to stop emotional eating when
you lighten up, rather than tighten up, on self-control. I'll explain
how to cut yourself some slack with food discipline without fear
that this will eliminate all remaining barriers that keep you from
going back to the other extreme.

To solve the mystery of unwanted emotional eating, the suspect
you're looking for is that part of your mind that, although you're not
consciously aware of it, has significant influence over your behavior.
Its goal may seem to be directly opposed to what you know you really
want, which is to eat less and lose weight. But if you view emotional
eating as a conflict between that part of you that wants to lose weight
and the side that rejects being controlled, then you can begin to listen to and understand the concerns of both sides. Each has a valid
position that must be understood before the conflict can be resolved.

The way to end unwanted eating is to first understand how it's
trying to work for you.

What This Book Adds to the Diet Book Shelf

Many books have been written about emotional eating, each
offering ways to explain the behavior and advice for how to overcome it. Writers on this topic typically point to the obvious fact

that the foods people usually binge on, like junk food, taste good, and that's why people binge on them. However, this overlooks the important fact that junk foods taste good because they're loaded with sugar and fat and are off-limits for someone on a diet. They may therefore be more desirable because they're forbidden fruit, and not just because they're tastier than salad.

The idea that emotional eating is driven by the pleasure-seeking hedonic motive also assumes that bingeing works as an all-purpose coping mechanism by providing a pleasurable experience to counteract bad feelings. The advice that logically follows from this is to identify the emotional experiences that trigger those negative feelings and address them directly instead of using food to feel better. This is often offered with the old chestnut, "It's not about what you're eating—it's about what's eating you!" That's not wrong; in fact, I also try to have my patients focus on the cause, rather than the behavior. But telling them to figure out what might be bothering them is too general. When pressed, everyone can point to some emotional issue that might be "eating" them on any given day, even if it may have little or no connection to their problem with food.

Not every desire to please must be eliminated to stop emotional eating. Just reducing the constant pressure to diet can be enough to eliminate unwanted compulsive eating. The sense that one must be on guard around food creates a constant underlying pressure that makes every eating opportunity a test of strength and will. I once asked a patient of mine to describe her experience of dieting. She thought for a moment and said, "At first, it's a feeling of being in complete control, and I feel that I can do this. But then it feels like walking on a tightrope, watching every step to avoid falling off. You can never relax and just eat what you want."

I thought that metaphor perfectly summed up the constant tension that my patients describe: they feel controlled by the diet, even though they choose to be on it. In their view, when they're on a diet, they're either on or off; there's nothing in between.

For those who feel a constant pressure to diet, even one small failure can be an opportunity to let go: "I already blew it, so I might as well eat whatever I want and I'll start the diet again tomorrow!" That moment of letting go is not a passive failure of resistance to temptation; it's an active choice to reject their usual compliance in order to satisfy a need for independence.

In 1943, the psychologist Kurt Lewin wrote, "There is nothing so practical as a good theory." An effective solution to any problem must start with a good theory to explain its cause and the mechanism that maintains it. When the theory is tested and proven effective, the solution can be used whenever the problem occurs. This is the case with emotional eating, where understanding why people do something that they really don't want to do is essential to stop the behavior. I'll propose an answer to explain why that happens and what you can do about it. Each key offers tools and exercises that will help you become more aware of what you're thinking and how you're thinking, and how to put that new awareness into practice.

The central idea in this book started with a very simple question that bothered me when I started treating people who came to me for help with overeating. As so many described their experience of eating during these episodes, they're barely tasting the food, much less enjoying what they eat, and then they feel worse, not better. So is there some other benefit they get that overrides the bad outcome?

I eventually came to answer that question and, as I had hoped, it proved to be very helpful to my patients, which inspired me to write this book. I have continued to develop this approach over the past 10 years and have used it in my practice with consistently successful outcomes, and have trained other clinicians to use it as well. My goal in writing this book is to make this help available to anyone who may have similar struggles with emotional eating.

When I began treating people with disordered eating, I already had 15 years of experience as a clinical psychologist, doing general psychotherapy with individuals and couples. I also taught some undergraduate college courses, including a course in health psychology, and it led me to focus more of my clinical work in that area.

I later took a position as a health psychologist in a medical weight management program. The patients I treated in this program were referred by my fellow clinicians, mostly physicians and dietitians. They recognized that of the people who came in for help with weight loss, many were already experienced life-long dieters who were very knowledgeable about diet and nutrition. These patients didn't need more information or professional advice on how to eat or lose weight. Instead, their issues tended to focus on their struggle with self-control, compulsive eating, and obsessive thoughts about food. They needed a psychologist to help them understand what's keeping them from doing what they already knew how to do.

When patients come to me for help with emotional eating, I always ask them for their thoughts about what they believe is causing the behavior. These are typical of the responses that I get:

"I just have no self-control."
"I sometimes eat to celebrate."
"I eat because I'm bored."
"I binge when I feel down."
"Sometimes I eat when I'm excited about losing some weight."

In fact, my patients have suggested so many different causes that they seem to cancel each other out. Happy and sad? Bored and excited? When pressed, anyone can point to some emotional issue that might be bothering them, but is it really the cause or is it hindsight? Trying to resolve a different issue each time they have an urge to binge can become a pointless game of whack-a-mole. A different cause can pop up to account for every new episode of emotional eating.

A parody of science news in the satirical newspaper, *The Onion*, reported "new findings" about the causes of binge eating. The headline was: *Study Links Binge Eating to Stress, Contentment, Depression, Joy, Boredom, Anger, Relaxation.* The report went on to describe the researchers' finding that "feelings of anxiety, self-confidence, embarrassment, grief, relief, hostility, composure, envy, pity, pride, and regret were also found to be linked to overeating."

As you can see, it can be hard to tell the difference between parody and reality. So, let's look more closely at the reality of emotional eating.

There are no statistics for the prevalence of emotional eating in the broad sense that I describe here. But we can get a sense of how common it is from the prevalence of the more narrowly defined diagnosis of binge eating disorder. More than 8% of American adults meet the criteria for binge eating disorder at some point in their lifetime. That's more than 15 million people in the United States alone. Outside of this country, those numbers may represent an additional 15 to 22 million people. And that only includes those who meet the strict criteria.

Consequently, there is a glut of books available to help people deal with this problem. So, you would be correct to ask, why add one more? *Eight Keys to End Emotional Eating* is intended to help those who have struggled with all forms of the problem, including unwanted overeating, binge eating disorder, and bulimia. In it, I present a new understanding of what causes this problem and I explain in detail how to use this understanding to overcome it.

Here is what this book is not: It is not a diet book, nor is it a guide to strengthen your willpower to fight the urge to eat things that aren't on your diet. It offers no meal plans, superfoods, low-cal recipes, or 28-day solutions. There are no foods that you must avoid. On the contrary, I have found that forbidding certain foods and then fighting the urge to eat them only makes the urge stronger, until you feel like you have to surrender to it, defeated. Instead, it's a guide to help you end the conflict that's going on internally and defuse the urge to binge at its start.

I'm also not a diet guru or nutritional expert; I'm a therapist with years of experience helping people achieve successful outcomes in their effort to overcome emotional eating. I don't tell my patients what they must do, whether they want to lose weight or just stop compulsive binge eating. Instead, I help them understand what has been getting in the way of stopping the unwanted behavior, and I offer guidance for how to do that. Consistent with the idea that an increased sense of autonomy is key to overcoming the problem, the choices they make must be their own. The steps outlined in this book are meant to serve the same purpose: to help you gain control over emotional eating by helping you identify and eliminate its source. If you eliminate the cause, you stop the effect.

But even if weight loss is your primary goal, it can only be achieved over the long term if you first address your tendency to use food as a coping tool. Otherwise, as you have probably experienced, any weight that you lose by dieting is almost certain to come back. That said, when my patients stop emotional eating, they usually do lose weight, because a lot of calories are consumed in those episodes of unrestrained eating.

Overview of the Book

As the title indicates, *8 Keys to End Emotional Eating* offers an eight-step guide to stop emotional eating and to reestablish a healthy mental attitude toward food. These steps can be thought of more broadly as a three-part program: how to understand the conflict that creates the urge for unwanted eating, how to resolve it, and how to adopt a healthy, enjoyable, and sustainable relationship with food. Each chapter is focused on one of the eight keys and is followed by exercises that will help you to relate the concepts discussed to your personal experience and apply them to your own struggle with food.

In Key 1, I explain what emotional eating is, the different terms often used to describe it, and what I mean by the terms used in the book. I also describe the types of behaviors and thinking patterns that emotional eaters engage in. I outline the four personality profiles that are most common among emotional eaters and explain how their thinking patterns and traits are related to their eating behavior. At the end of that chapter, you'll be able to do a self-assessment and see if you recognize your own personality style among the four that I describe.

Key 2 explains how our bodies are well adapted to determine what, when, and how much we want to eat. Understanding this can help you find your healthy weight if you can just allow your body to do its job. This chapter will help you learn how to regain trust in your judgment and intuition about eating, and stop trying to manage your body through dieting and food selection.

Key 3 describes practical strategies for changes that you can make that affect your regular eating routine and food choices. This chapter examines the most common types of habits—behavioral and mental—that can get in the way of normal eating and offers suggestions and exercises to modify them.

In Key 4, I discuss the central question of what motivates emotional eating and the obstacles that get in the way of stopping the behavior. I present a framework for understanding the cause of emotional eating that's based on the tension we maintain between our need to feel accepted and our need for autonomy. I explain the effort we make to balance those needs and how, when pressure to conform for the sake of acceptance disrupts that balance, it can lead to defiant behavior like emotional eating.

Key 5 focuses on how to resolve the conflict between the need for belonging and the need for autonomy discussed in Key 4. I explain how both sides of this conflict are each trying to help you in different ways. Their efforts, however, can make them feel like adversaries fighting a tug-of-war, ultimately leading to emotional eating. I'll explain how, by adapting techniques used to negotiate conflict resolution, you can engage in a process of internal negotiation between these two sides of you to work together on your behalf. Reducing the conflict restores internal balance, making the need for defiant eating unnecessary. This will allow you to change the effect (emotional eating) by stopping its cause (the tug-of-war).

In Key 6, I describe the three types of psychological coping, and how a quick-fix coping strategy that focuses on short-term relief of emotional discomfort can make the problem of emotional eating worse. I explain more effective coping responses. Understanding this misalignment between the problem and the coping response can help you identify alternative strategies that are a better fit for overcoming the problem.

Key 7 explains how perceptions can be distorted by the way we filter our experiences. Awareness of your go-to filters can help you question certain beliefs that trigger the impulse to binge. Acknowledging these thoughts while challenging the beliefs and initial assumptions will allow you to choose alternative interpretations of events that might otherwise lead to binge behavior.

In Key 8, I explain how learning to accept thoughts about eating without fear of acting on them can transform your relationship with food from one of anxiety and guilt to an experience of pleasure and genuine enjoyment. The goal of this chapter is to provide ideas that can help you put the changes discussed in the book into action and make them practical and sustainable for the rest of your life.

I tried to organize these key points about ending emotional eating in a way that makes sense, but they're not meant to be a recipe that you have to follow in any particular order. They're separate (though often related) ideas that address the questions and obstacles to change that have come up most frequently in my work with emotional eaters. I have found that these ideas have been the most useful in helping my patients overcome their struggle with emotional eating.

I believe that understanding these key points will provide guidance and a sense of hope for living a life that is not dominated by food concerns or fear of social disapproval. I hope that it will help you enjoy the simple pleasures of a satisfying and healthy lifelong relationship with food.

Are You an Emotional Eater?

If you have concerns about your overeating behavior but aren't sure if this book addresses that problem, you can find out by answering the following questions. First, let's determine the approximate frequency of your overeating episodes by circling one of the three choices under the first item. Then read the following statements and circle the response that most closely describes how the statement lines up with your experience:

I have episodes of eating very large amounts of food, beyond what I would normally need or want to eat . . .

Less than monthly   Several times a month   Weekly or more

In the following set of questions, I'll use the term "binge eating" to refer to this behavior:

1. Episodes of binge eating cause me to feel very distressed.

   Disagree   Somewhat disagree   Somewhat agree   Agree

2. When I am not binge eating, I try to be very in control of what I eat.

    Disagree Somewhat disagree Somewhat agree Agree

3. I'm more likely to binge after eating something that I feel I shouldn't.

    Disagree Somewhat disagree Somewhat agree Agree

4. There are certain foods that I will not bring into my house.

    Disagree Somewhat disagree Somewhat agree Agree

5. Binge episodes usually follow a period of strict dieting.

    Disagree Somewhat disagree Somewhat agree Agree

6. When I think about eating something bad, I usually try to stop that thought.

    Disagree Somewhat disagree Somewhat agree Agree

7. I categorize most of what I eat as either good foods or bad foods.

    Disagree Somewhat disagree Somewhat agree Agree

8. After I binge, I feel like I must recommit to dieting.

    Disagree Somewhat disagree Somewhat agree Agree

9. While I'm bingeing, I don't really enjoy what I'm eating.

    Disagree Somewhat disagree Somewhat agree Agree

10. I only binge if no one else is around.

   Disagree Somewhat disagree Somewhat agree Agree

11. I often binge when I'm feeling resentful about dieting.

   Disagree Somewhat disagree Somewhat agree Agree

12. The act of binge eating feels rebellious.

   Disagree Somewhat disagree Somewhat agree Agree

The first question establishes the approximate frequency of binge eating episodes, and the rest of the questions describe the thoughts and feelings that accompany the eating behavior. The kind of emotional eating that I refer to in this book involves the latter. Each item from 1 to 12 is scored from 0 to 3; Disagree = 0, Somewhat disagree = 1, Somewhat agree = 2, Agree = 3.

If you have occasional eating episodes in which you consume what you consider to be a very large amount of food, but they occur with a frequency of once a month or less, and you score below 10, you may need to learn more about making healthy eating choices without feeling deprived, and might benefit from speaking with a professional who specializes in a non-diet approach to eating and nutrition. You're probably not an emotional eater, but you may find the information in this book helpful.

If you experience binge eating episodes more than once a month, and score between 10 and 19, you may have a pattern of emotional eating and would probably benefit from reading this book. If you experience binge episodes that occur once a week or more, and score above 20, you are the type of emotional eater that this book was written for. I hope you'll find it helpful.

Identify Your Eating Patterns

Recognizing your routine eating patterns is the first step in overcoming emotional eating. One useful way to begin the process of examining these eating habits is to apply the five Ws of information-gathering: What, When, Why, Where, and Who (or perhaps, better, With Whom). Think about your typical daily food routines (not the episodes of emotional eating), beginning with When:

When:

- After you wake up in the morning, what's the first thing you eat?
- How long after you get up?
- Do you have between-meal snacks? If so, when?
- Did you snack between dinner and bedtime?
- Do you eat at scheduled meal times?
- Do you tend to graze through the day instead of having regular meal times?
- Do you get up in the middle of the night to eat?

What:

- If you eat breakfast in the morning, what do you usually have?
- What portion sizes (or how many servings) do you take?
- Do you eat everything on your plate, regardless of hunger/satisfaction?
- How many fast food meals do you eat per week?
- Do you make an effort to choose foods that you believe are good for you?
- What qualities make you think of food as good or bad: e.g., calories, fat, carbs, health benefits, other?
- Do you usually prepare your own meals, or do you go for convenience?

- When you choose convenience, what do you usually choose: e.g., eat out, order-in, microwave, other?
- What do you doing while you eat: read, watch TV, work at the computer, or do you focus only on what you're eating?
- What do you usually eat for snacks?

Why:

- What typically prompts your decision to eat a regular snack or meal: hunger cues, emotional cues, time of day, other?
- What emotional cues (internal) tend to trigger a binge episode?
- What situations (external) tend to trigger thoughts about bingeing?
- Do you eat just because you happen to see some food that's available?
- Does being in a social situation affect your desire to eat or not eat regardless of hunger?
- If you feel like bingeing, or even just to eating something you ordinarily would avoid, do you try to find some reason or excuse to feel better about doing it?

Where:

- If you eat breakfast at home, do you eat in your kitchen, dining room, family room, bedroom, car, office, other?
- If you work from home, is lunch the same as breakfast?
- If not, where do you eat lunch: the kitchen, family room, car, office, cafeteria, restaurant, other?
- In a typical week, how often do you eat dinner while sitting at a kitchen or dining room table?
- Where do you most often eat any meal?

- How many meals each day do you read while watching TV or working at the computer?
- Do you usually eat standing up or sitting down?

With Whom:

- Do you usually eat with others or by yourself?
- When you eat around other people what effect does it have on the choice you make?
- Do you tend to make better choices and limit how much you eat or are you influenced in one way or another by the choices others around you make?
- Does eating alone influence either what or how much you eat?
- Do you usually eat with others or by yourself?
- When you eat around other people what effect does it have on the choice you make?
- Do you tend to make better choices and limit how much you eat or are you influenced in one way or another by the choices others around you make?
- Does eating alone influence either what or how much you eat?

Reflecting on Your Patterns of Emotional Eating

Beyond reviewing your eating-related behavior patterns, as in the 5W exercise above, self-reflection can be very helpful to understand the thoughts and feelings that surround emotional eating. You may want to come back to these questions after reading Key 1.

1. What is your theory to explain what causes you to eat when you don't want to?

_____

_____

_____

2. What thoughts or rationalizations go on in your mind just before you act on the impulse to eat something or some amount of food that you know you'll regret later?

_____

_____

_____

3. What types of food do you typically think about when you feel like emotional eating? Are they ever foods that you feel would usually be okay to eat?

_____

_____

_____

4. What kind of thoughts do you have after bingeing? Include thoughts like regrets, resolutions for the future, or anything else that comes to mind following a binge episode.

_____

_____

_____

5. Now review your answers to the 5W questions and your reflections about your eating patterns. Then write a summary paragraph that describes, in your own words, when, what, where, why, and with whom you eat. Include information from the reflections about your thoughts before.

_____

_____

_____

_____

_____

_____

_____

_____

_____

_____

_____

KEY 1

GET A FIX ON
EMOTIONAL EATING

What Is Emotional Eating?

To understand how to overcome emotional eating, it's important to first clarify three key questions: What is it? Whom does it affect? Why does it occur?

In this chapter, I describe the behaviors and eating patterns that differentiate emotional eating from more benign forms of overeating, and the ways that it differs from other eating disorders. Then I discuss the shared characteristics of those who struggle with the problem, focusing particularly on the behavioral patterns and thinking styles that are most common among them. I also explain how a better understanding of those characteristics might offer important clues for how to overcome it. Later, in Key 4, I address that last question, which is to understand the motivation for engaging in it. This question underlies the central focus of this book and is what differentiates the framework that I use from other approaches to treating emotional eating. For now, I focus on describing what it is and whom it tends to affect.

I use the term *emotional eating* for two reasons: first, to include people whose eating disorder is atypical or below the threshold for the diagnosis of binge eating disorder or bulimia nervosa. If you're concerned about your eating and find that it doesn't meet the diagnostic manual's definition, you shouldn't assume that your problem would be dismissed. You may have a persistent pattern of eating that's unwanted and out of your control, which is itself emotionally upsetting—apart from any stress that may have triggered the behavior. That's a problem that needs to be addressed. Second, the term *emotional eating* is also meant to broaden the focus from the behavior itself, such as bingeing and/or purging, to highlight the emotional distress that results from the behavior.

The types of eating behaviors that people often consider to be a problem can range from benign overeating or choosing to eat higher-calorie comfort foods to more serious problems like binge eating disorder and bulimia nervosa. Using Figure 1.1 as the frame of reference, most of my patients, and those of you who will benefit from this book, tend to struggle with behaviors in the emotional eating and binge eating disorder range.

FIGURE 1.1 – Emotional eating from benign to disordered

Comfort eating	Stress eating	Emotional eating	Binge eating disorder	Bulimia Nervosa

There are formal definitions for the more serious forms of emotional eating based on the severity and frequency of the behavior. For diagnostic purposes, binge eating disorder is defined by the following criteria:

1. repeated instances, at least weekly for three months or more, of eating a very large amount of food in a discrete period of time;
2. during these episodes, feeling compelled to eat, as if you're not in control of the decision to eat, the amount you eat, or when to stop eating;
3. feeling very distressed about this pattern of eating.

Plus, most of the following behaviors:

4. eating large amounts of food even when you're not hungry, eating
    quickly, eating until you're uncomfortably full, eating alone out
    of shame, and feeling disgusted, depressed, or guilty after eating.

Although many of my patients certainly do meet the criteria for
the diagnosis, many do not. The standard that I consider relevant
to define emotional eating is that the individual reports a recurrent
pattern of having an unwanted urge to eat, is preoccupied and conflicted about it, then acts on that urge. They don't know why they
do it, and feel distressed by their loss of control. Those aspects of
emotional eating are more telling than the quantity they eat.

On the basis of behavior alone, the distinction between binge
eating and normal overeating may appear to be only a difference
of degree. For a long time, binge eating was assumed to afflict only
obese overeaters, as if that would be the only way to explain their
weight gain. However, we now know that most individuals with
obesity do not engage in recurrent binge eating episodes. Similarly,
the vast majority of emotional eaters, including those who meet all
the formal criteria for binge eating disorder, are not obese.

Bulimia nervosa is an eating disorder that also involves cycles
of binge eating, but these episodes tend to be followed by purging.
This syndrome shares all the criteria of binge eating disorder, with
the addition of compensatory behavior, typically self-induced vomit-
ing. But it can also be any behavior intended to undo the binge episode, such as the use of laxatives, fasting, or extreme exercise. Binge
eating also occurs in about half of cases presenting with anorexia
nervosa, which is extremely restrictive eating or self-starvation.

Even after bulimia was recognized as a distinct eating disorder in 1979, binge eating without purging was well known to be
far more common, estimated to affect three times the number of
people diagnosed with anorexia and bulimia combined. In spite

of its prevalence, it was another 34 years before binge eating disorder was officially recognized as a diagnosis with the publication of the fifth edition of the *Diagnostic and Statistical Manual of Mental Disorders* (*DSM-5*) in 2013 (American Psychiatric Association, 2013). Although they're considered to be different disorders, for the purposes of this book, bulimia and binge eating are both types of what I consider to be emotional eating. The advice offered here would be equally helpful to those who want to overcome any form of this behavior.

Among adults, binge eating disorder is roughly twice as common among women than men. In my work with those who struggle with emotional eating, I've found that the differences between men and women in terms of the psychological causes of the problem tend to reflect the same ratio. Men appear to be less concerned about the pressure to lose weight than they are about other external pressures like work and relationships. This is most likely related to the disproportionate diet pressure and body shaming that women in our culture experience compared to men. Women may therefore identify more closely with many of the diet-related examples that I offer in this book. However, the men whom I've treated for emotional eating identify with the broader experience of feeling controlled and have benefited equally from understanding its role in unwanted eating.

Emotional Eating and Bariatric Surgery

I mentioned above that most emotional eaters are not obese. However, among those who have struggled with obesity, some have opted to undergo bariatric surgery. The decision about whether to have surgery or not is very individual, and I won't make any general recommendations about that. However, I will offer some observations about patients whom I have worked with after having had the surgery and the impact of emotional eating on the outcome over time.

Contrary to the comments I've heard from some about their thoughts while considering the procedure, bariatric surgery for obesity is not taking the easy way out. There is nothing easy about making the decision to undergo a surgical procedure or taking on the commitment required to go through months of preparation, psychological evaluation, nutritional education, a strict presurgery diet, and postsurgery behavior change. This last step is the one that's most difficult for those who struggle with emotional eating. It's also the most important, because if the psychological component is not addressed, the benefits of the surgery can be completely undone.

Several different types of bariatric surgery are currently being done. The most common ones are gastric sleeve surgery and gastric bypass surgery. These work primarily by reducing the size of the stomach, making the patient feel full sooner while eating, and by reducing the hunger-causing hormones secreted by the stomach. Patients typically lose up to 70% of their excess body weight within 18 months to two years.

However, about a year or more postsurgery, up to 30% of these patients regain at least some of that weight. The amount regained varies widely, from only a small amount to all of it. This weight regain is usually caused by the stomach stretching back to its original capacity, which undoes the effect of feeling full after eating, allowing the person to eat more and, as a result, regain weight.

A certain amount of stomach stretching and weight regain is normal after surgery even for those with perfect diets and eating habits. But the surgery does nothing to change the psychological issues that contributed to the problem to begin with. As I've told my patients, it only changes how your body processes what you eat, not how you think about it. So if you were accustomed to eating beyond your stomach's capacity, that habit may continue even after surgery. Although the amount you will eat is much less than before the surgery, over the course of about a year, your stomach could gradually return to its previous size, and the benefits will be lost.

Most insurance companies require a presurgery psychological evaluation, in large part to assess the likelihood of continued disordered eating affecting the outcome of the surgery. In addition to this evaluation, I would recommend a follow-up psychological evaluation after around the six-month mark for anyone undergoing the surgery. That's because predicting adherence to recommendations prior to surgery can be a sucker's bet for even the most experienced evaluator. The real test is an assessment of how the patient adjusts in the first year after surgery, preferably before there is any significant weight regain. If the patient is experiencing difficulty with emotional eating during that period, it's essential to seek out psychotherapy with someone experienced and well qualified in the treatment of emotional eating. The bottom line is that bariatric surgery will almost certainly help you lose weight in the first year or so, but it does not cure binge (or any other) eating disorder, and the benefits of surgery can be nullified.

I'll add one more point on the topic of bariatric surgery that's relevant to understanding emotional eating in general. I've seen many patients who have struggled with severe binge eating for many years, and lost weight after surgery and maintained it. Although from a medical point of view the intended outcome was good, they developed problems with impulse control in other areas, such as alcohol abuse, sexual compulsions, and gambling, among others. My own experience with these patients is anecdotal, but it has been reported in the medical and psychological literature as a widely observed phenomenon.

This *transfer addiction*, as it's often called, remains a controversial issue, but as I pointed out in the introduction and explain in detail in Key 4, the motivation for emotional eating is not about the food but rather the need to assert autonomy by defying some rules. This could explain how preventing one type of unwanted behavior could lead to a similar pattern with some other social or personal taboo. It's like squeezing one end of a partially inflated balloon; if the behavior is prevented in one area, it could just show up somewhere else. Although more research needs to be done about this, I believe that this shift from emotional eating to another unwanted behavior following surgery is a real issue that anyone who is considering having bariatric surgery should be aware of and discuss with a professional who has experience working with this problem.

Can Food Be an Addiction?

On the topic of behavioral addictions, I'll address one presumed cause for emotional eating that I find very unhelpful: the belief that food itself can be addictive.

Using the term *addiction* to describe emotional eating isn't wrong if it's meant as a metaphor, as in, "I'm just addicted to this chocolate cake!" Resisting an unwanted impulse to eat can be just as difficult as resisting any chemical addiction. But sometimes, when the term *addiction* is used in the context of emotional eating, it's meant to be taken literally: that the behavior is caused by a physical dependence on a substance, in this case, food.

I have a problem with that use of the term because it blurs an important distinction between psychological compulsions and chemical dependency, and ignoring that distinction can get in the way of overcoming the behavior. A compulsion refers to a behavior that you feel you must do to bring some psychological relief; an addiction refers to physical dependence on a chemical substance that your body needs, and without which you'll experience potentially dangerous physical reactions.

Addiction to a chemical substance has three unique characteristics:

- The first is that it involves a substance that is normally not used by the body, nor is it necessary for survival, but it has a chemical effect on the reward center of the brain when it's introduced.

- The second is that when it's used repeatedly to trigger the reward center, the brain develops a tolerance to the substance, which becomes less effective in producing the rewarding response. At this point, the user may increase the amount used until it produces the effect again.
- The third is that after the brain has become accustomed to the substance, it becomes dependent on it. The reason for this is that being without it is now abnormal, which will cause the person to experience symptoms of withdrawal. This can range from a mild headache (like caffeine withdrawal), to tremors, seizures, delirium, and even death caused by withdrawal from prolonged, heavy use of certain addictive substances, including alcohol.

Let's see how a psychological compulsion like emotional eating compares to these characteristics of addiction. Food, of course, naturally has a chemical makeup, and it's rewarding to the brain. That's important because it encourages us to seek out needed calories, which, for almost all of human history, were scarce. But since the body relies on food for nutrition as a necessary part of its functioning, it does not meet the first criterion of introducing a nonvital chemical substance to the body. For the same reason, food doesn't alter the way our brain and body normally function, so we can't develop a tolerance to it. So it fails the second criterion too. Since food is always necessary to sustain life, there can be no new normal state the body must first get used to and then withdraw from. Strike three.

The editors of the *DSM-5* conclude in their introduction to the section Substance-Related and Addictive Disorders that "groups of repetitive behaviors, which some term *behavioral addictions* . . . are not included because at this time there is insufficient peer-reviewed evidence" (American Psychiatric Association, 2013, p. 481).

Beyond the lack of evidence, it's important to be careful about using the term *addiction* when referring to emotional eating, because it could imply that the treatment should follow the model for treating a true chemical dependency. An important part of addiction treatment is to abstain from the substance, which is, of course, impossible with food. As I'll explain later on, even trying to abstain from certain foods that are designated as off-limits (like sugar or refined flour) can make the problem of emotional eating worse. That's exactly what most people who chronically diet feel they must do, and it's a big part of the reason that diets fail.

Four Types of Emotional Eaters

In my work with emotional eaters over the years, I've seen many different types of people, each with their own story to tell and their unique experience of the world. However, I've also noted that there are patterns that tend to repeat. I've identified four types of personality patterns among emotional eaters that I tend to see most frequently. Although this isn't meant to be an exhaustive description of the variety of behavior patterns among emotional eaters, and there is a fair amount of overlap between these types, they're sufficiently distinct to illustrate the more common behavior patterns that are associated with emotional eating. You may be able to identify one or two of these patterns in yourself:

- *The Appeaser,* who is uncomfortable saying no to others, but then feels taken advantage of and resentful of their requests
- *The Imposter,* who privately feels unworthy of achievement or success and fears that the slightest mistake might reveal their secret incompetence
- *The Perfectionist,* who believes that making a mistake is a sign of failure, or at least failure to stay on course to their success goals and drive to achieve
- *The Suppressor,* who avoids expressing feelings due to fear that it might lead to a loss of emotional control

Below I describe each of them in more detail and provide case examples. As you read the descriptions, you may be able to recognize how the descriptions of these types match up with some of your own thinking and behavior.

The Appeaser

The Appeaser may be the most common type among emotional eaters. Appeasers tend to put their own needs aside, if necessary, when someone asks for a favor. A request for help feels more like an obligation, and they usually end up with too much on their plate, figuratively and literally.

Arlene was one patient of mine who typifies the Appeaser. She was a single, semiretired consultant with an active social life, who managed to fit volunteer work into her schedule as well. When her friend Sandra had surgery, she relied on Arlene and others in her circle of friends to do errands for her while she recovered.

They all helped her initially, but Sandra continued to rely on Arlene even after she could do more for herself. Arlene complied with Sandra's requests and even gave her errands a higher priority than items on her own to-do list. Privately, though, Arlene felt increasingly resentful, and her episodes of binge eating increased as well.

When we discussed this in our sessions, Arlene had difficulty explaining why she felt so compelled to say yes. "Rationally, I know she won't stop being my friend, but even when I decide that I won't do the next thing she asks, I still can't bring myself to say no."

Arlene's all-or-nothing way of thinking is a significant feature of emotional eaters, as I'll describe in more detail in Key 7. It's revealed in her feeling that a simple request for help is the same as a demand. It's also reflected in her belief that saying no can risk losing the friendship. Just as there is no room to politely decline a request, there's no forgiveness for rejecting it. For an Appeaser, a request for help feels no less controlling than a demand.

This is an example of how this type of thinking is often coupled with a strong need for acceptance among people who use binge eating to cope emotionally. When the stress and resentment of having to sacrifice their own needs to take care of others becomes unbearable, food compensates for their self-restraint in those other ways.

Appeaser Self-Test

If you answer yes to more than three of the following statements, you may identify with much of what I described as Appeaser qualities:

1. I have a hard time asking for help from others.
2. I often feel like I am being used.
3. I worry about being rejected even by individuals I don't like.
4. I worry too much about hurting other people's feelings.
5. I put my own needs aside when others ask me to do something.
6. I'm overly concerned about what people think of me.
7. I feel guilty when I say no.
8. Friends have told me that I'm a people pleaser.

The Imposter

Most people who have difficulty with emotional eating are successful at what they do professionally, and in other areas of their lives as well. As is true of anyone who reliably performs well at a job or on any task, their success reflects their true ability. To paraphrase Forrest Gump, successful is as successful does.

Despite their demonstrated success, however, I have found that many of my patients see themselves as frauds. They question their competence and tend to ascribe their success to luck and to the extra effort they put in to cover their deception. They believe that it's only a matter of time before that cover is blown. The result is that they tend to be overly vigilant in everything they do out of fear of making mistakes.

When Imposters complete a project or give a presentation, for example, their response is not satisfaction or a sense of accomplishment for a job well-done. Instead, they feel relieved that they've just dodged another bullet. Whenever they have an opportunity to shine, it's spoiled by the anxiety of being exposed, so they're always just holding their breath until the work day is over. After that, they often go home and binge.

Ruth is an executive assistant in a busy accounting firm. While she was a student, she lived with her parents, who were recent immigrants, and worked part-time to help support them. During her last semester of school, her father was laid off from his job, and Ruth had to put her education on hold to work full-time.

When she first applied for a job in the accounting firm, she felt unqualified because she lacked a degree, but she did well on the screening tests and impressed the executives in her interviews. She was hired even though she didn't finish college, and her energy, intelligence, and exceptional work ethic were soon recognized. Before Ruth finished her first year at this job, she was promoted to oversee the administrative assistants and eventually became the executive assistant to the managing partner.

Despite her outstanding performance reviews and promotions, she still saw herself as a college dropout who was pretending to be qualified for her position and was afraid that the smallest mistake would expose her as unqualified.

When she went home after work, Ruth felt emotionally spent, but also liberated from the pressure she had been feeling all day. That was when her thoughts would turn to food and what she could binge on—without having to worry about what other people were thinking.

Imposter Self-Test

If you answer yes to more than three of the following statements, you may identify with much of what I described as Imposter qualities:

1. I feel that I have to work harder just to maintain the expectations that others have for me.
2. I usually feel that any success I have is just due to luck.
3. When I do something well, I feel a sense of relief rather than accomplishment.
4. I feel that I don't deserve it when I get good feedback for my work.
5. I often worry that people will realize that I'm not really as smart as they think I am.
6. I usually feel that others around me are more intelligent or capable than I am.
7. I have a hard time accepting praise for my work or abilities.
8. I don't offer my own opinions or ideas when I should.

The Perfectionist

There are two types of perfectionist: one is very exacting about getting the details right because these people take personal pride in their work, even if no one else notices. They're driven by a passion for their work and take pride in the final product turning out just as they envisioned. Examples of this kind of perfectionist would be the chef who spends time fussing over a drop of sauce while plating a dish, or the writer who spends time making sure that every comma is placed correctly.

The other type of perfectionist is motivated more by fear of failure than by passion for their work. Examples of this type are the straight-A high school student who's unreasonably upset about an A-minus and how it will affect getting into a good college, or the professional who's distressed by a performance review that rates her as merely "above expectations" rather than "well above."

Perfectionists who are emotional eaters tend to be driven more by fear of failure than by passion. Like Imposters, who fear exposure of their secret identity, Perfectionists consider a good day as one in which they can get through without slipping up. They're also more likely to experience relief rather than accomplishment at the end of what they define as a successful day.

Failing, in their view, happens when they put a real effort into achieving some goal and still don't meet their own expectations. This leaves open a loophole. By not putting in a full effort, they can blame the apparent failure on external circumstances instead of ability. Therefore, they often procrastinate starting on a project, or fail to study or rehearse, so they can attribute a potential subpar performance to a lack of effort rather than ability.

Perfectionists may be particularly hard on themselves after an episode of binge eating, after which they'll tend to be more restrictive than usual about what they eat. One patient of mine maintained a very low-calorie diet, weighing, counting, and recording everything she ate. At night, before setting out her clothes for the next morning, she would add up the calories from her food diary. If the total was within her daily limit, she would reward herself by choosing clothes from the part of her closet where she kept her favorite, newest, and most flattering things to wear. But if the total was even slightly over the limit, she felt unworthy of feeling good about herself and would choose items from the section where she kept old, worn out, and unflattering outfits.

She worked hard to control her urge to overeat, but about once a week, usually after she gave in to some small craving that wasn't part of her diet plan, she binged until she felt physically sick. When that happened, she reduced her daily food ration even further for as long as she felt was appropriate to make up for the extra calories consumed during the lapse.

Perfectionist Self-Test

If you answer yes to more than three of the following statements, you may identify with much of what I described as Perfectionist qualities:

1. People tell me that I have unrealistic expectations for myself.
2. If I don't do a job perfectly, I can be very hard on myself.
3. I believe that there's a right way and a wrong way to do most things.
4. I have difficulty making decisions because I'm afraid I might make the wrong choice.
5. If I start a diet, I intend to follow it perfectly.
6. If I eat something that's not on a diet, I may as well give up and start again another day.
7. I'll think more about a mistake I've made than something that I've done well.
8. I often put off getting started on things or leave them unfinished if I think they won't turn out as well as I'd like.

The Suppressor

Suppressors tend to deal with negative emotions internally, without acknowledging that they're feeling angry, overwhelmed, or anxious, or need help from anyone else. Often, they're not even consciously aware of those feelings. They may not have the tools to express themselves emotionally, or they may not feel comfortable doing so.

Typically, Suppressors are afraid of expressing their anger. They believe that if they give voice to negative emotions of any kind, they may lose control of how they express it, resulting in a potentially destructive and humiliating outburst. In addition, they're concerned that showing how they feel makes them appear weak or overly emotional. Their fear is that this might lead to rejection and social isolation.

When they do finally express themselves, it's likely that whatever triggered them to say something was the last straw—in line with the accumulated emotions they had been bottling up, and disproportionate to the immediate situation. It's similar to bingeing on food, except that now they binge on anger. Instead of learning not to bottle up their negative emotions, their take-away lesson is to double down on suppressing their feelings or to express them through episodes of uncontrolled eating.

Whether it's forbidden anger or forbidden food, the uncontrolled nature of the behavior allows them to feel liberated from the effort at self-control by letting go of self-censorship and self-denial. The difference is that open and direct expression of anger has immediate social consequences, while binge eating in private is socially safe.

Kendra is a single mother and the only female executive in her company. Her job has very high visibility, and she's always working on at least one or two projects with hard deadlines. As the only female executive, Kendra feels she must always maintain her emotional composure, regardless of the pressure she's under, to avoid being stereotyped as an emotional woman. She had binged occasionally in the past, but the episodes began to increase in frequency to several times a week when she was going through a divorce. She describes her eating as "out of control," and she works out daily trying to maintain her weight.

Between her job and her responsibilities as a single mother, she has no social life and no close friends to confide in, and is too overwhelmed to find time to speak to her only sister. She's gotten so used to pushing down her feelings that she does it even when she's alone. "I haven't cried in a long time," she told me. Her only outlet, she explained, is to let go when she eats.

Suppressor Self-Test

If you answer yes to more than three of the following statements, you may identify with much of what I described as Suppressor qualities:

1. I try to keep my emotions to myself.
2. I believe that other people see me as unemotional.
3. If I do feel angry or upset, I make an effort not to show it.
4. I lose my temper when I can't hold back angry feelings.
5. I'm concerned how people will judge me if I express my feelings openly.
6. I'm afraid that I'd lose control if I expressed any anger at all.
7. When I do lose my temper, it feels kind of liberating in the moment.
8. I control my emotions mainly by holding them in.

Shared Traits of Emotional Eaters

Having described the unique traits and patterns that distinguish each of these types of emotional eaters, let's look at what they have in common. The first shared trait that stands out is the tendency toward binary thinking, which is apparent in the descriptions of each of the four types. As I explain in Key 7, binary thinking describes how most emotional eaters tend to view the world in all-or-nothing terms.

They think about food as either good or bad—not based on how it tastes, but in categorical terms that refer to how likely it is to cause weight gain, how unhealthy it is, and even as a moral judgment that reflects on themselves if they eat it: "I was good today because I only had a salad for lunch"—and, of course, the opposite if it was followed by dessert. Their fear of slipping up on their diet is equally extreme; it's not a one-time lapse but the start of unending weight gain. Catastrophic slippery slopes are an ever-present danger.

Beyond how they think is what they think; what are the common food-related issues that emotional eaters think about? I'll focus on three of their shared concerns that play an important role in emotional eating.

First, emotional eaters who fit the descriptions in this chapter feel the need to restrict what they eat, whether they're actively engaged in a formal diet program or just feel that they must try harder to control what they eat. Although they want the results that they hope will come from cutting calories, they experience this restriction as a necessary, even if unwanted, obligation.

Second, they try to control some feared behavior or emotion that they believe will threaten their status in their relationships with others: The Appeaser hides the resentment she feels toward others who take advantage of her kindness. The threat is the loss of a relationship. The Imposter is hiding what she believes to be the fact that she's unqualified to do the job that she nevertheless is doing well. The threat is exposure as a fraud and public humiliation. Similarly, the Perfectionist is hiding her perceived lack of competence to accomplish the tasks that others can do without sweating over the details. The threat is failure and its consequences. Finally, the Suppressor must maintain an emotional mask to control what she believes will be the eruption of her uncontrollable rage. The threat is unleashing her destructive emotional impulses.

Finally, each type tends to view their emotional state as a ticking time bomb that must either be defused and disabled or, failing that, safely detonated in a controlled explosion. Binge eating is a discharge of that pent-up emotional energy and is the common denominator shared by all types of emotional eaters. Episodes of emotional eating temporarily relieves some of this pressure that they carry with them in their daily lives.

Self-Assessment Discussion

1. Based on the assessments, which of the types do you
   most closely match up with? Choose more than one if
   appropriate:

   ____ Appeaser
   ____ Imposter
   ____ Perfectionist
   ____ Suppressor

2. Write an example of an experience that fits those
   patterns:

   Appeaser: _____
   _____
   _____
   _____

   Imposter: _____
   _____
   _____
   _____

   Perfectionist: _____
   _____
   _____
   _____

   Suppressor: _____
   _____
   _____
   _____

3. How did you think, feel, and respond at the time?

   a. Thinking: _____

   _____

   _____

   _____

   b. Feeling: _____

   _____

   _____

   _____

   c. Responding: _____

   _____

   _____

   _____

4. How might you have handled it differently in any or all three of those ways? _____

   _____

   _____

   _____

KEY 2

BREAK THE DIET MENTALITY

The Eating Instinct

In 1939, Chicago pediatrician Dr. Clara Davis presented a paper at a conference that summarized the results of a research program she had begun a decade earlier. Her goal was to learn how children who were just beginning to eat solid food would eat when they could choose foods freely. She set up a residential care program for single mothers and their newly weaned infants and recorded everything the children ate for up to four and a half years.

The children were offered a variety of over 30 different foods to choose from, and the only rule was that they had to choose for themselves, without adult guidance or encouragement. "The nurses' orders were to sit quietly by, spoon in hand, and make no motion," she wrote (Davis, 1928). The children could have chosen to undereat or overeat, or to eat an unbalanced diet by choosing foods naturally high in starch, fat or sugar, for example.

When the study was over, Dr. Davis found that the average daily calories consumed by the children over each six-month period were always within the recommended nutritional limits for their age. The only exceptions were noteworthy: children who were malnourished or suffering from vitamin deficiencies when they joined the study took in more calories than average for the first six months.

Like the toddlers in Clara Davis's study, there was a time when we were all experts on what we should eat, even though we knew nothing about nutrition. Babies eat when they're hungry and then turn their heads away when they're not. They know what food they like, and they'll spit it out if they don't. And they stop when they've had enough. But as they get older, children are taught to override those instincts. We've all been told that we should eat good foods that we don't like, and avoid bad foods that we do like, that we must not spoil our appetites, and that we must finish everything on our plate.

I'll summarize those lessons: Don't eat what you like. Do eat what you don't like. Don't eat when you're hungry. Do eat when you're full. Our nutritional education is now complete and we don't have the slightest idea how to eat normally. Most importantly, we no longer trust our innate eating instincts. This uncertainty about how and what to eat makes people vulnerable to fad diets of every kind. You look for definitive answers and clear direction, but you feel bewildered by information overload. Nutritional studies published in prestigious medical journals claim breakthrough findings and make headlines in the media, only to be contradicted by later research. Should you make different choices or wait for more studies to confirm one conclusion or the other? Understandably, you wonder, if the experts can't figure it out, how can I?

While you feel confused and impatient for practical answers, diet promoters speak to you with great confidence, promising guaranteed success and quick results. They understand that you're looking for someone who can tell you with absolute certainty what you should eat in order to lose weight. But dieting is a trap and this promise is the irresistible bait that lures you in. It's very seductive for those who struggle with eating and have concerns about their weight. In this chapter, I'll explain the role that this diet mentality plays in the development and maintenance of the emotional eating cycle. I'll also explain why understanding this connection and how to resist it is one of the first keys to overcoming emotional eating. I'll begin by describing an extreme version of the diet mentality that brings it into sharp focus.

Precision Eating

There are some dieters whose reliance on rules goes beyond typical diet planning. It involves strict avoidance of anything considered by the dieter to be fattening or unhealthy food. This is a type of disordered eating that's been described by physician Steven Bratman (2000) as *orthorexia*. He introduced the term (which means correct eating) in his book *Health Food Junkies* to describe a pattern of disordered eating characterized by perfectionism. I think of it as a form of overly controlled precision eating. It involves a strictly selective approach to eating that's based on some criterion, like perceived health effects (as opposed to personal preference). It may involve eliminating anything from particular ingredients to entire food groups. For such dieters, eating comes close to a ritualistic obsession that can take over their lives.

Here are some common signs of orthorexic behavior:

- Compulsive checking of ingredient lists and nutritional labels
- Cutting out entire food groups for supposed health benefits rather than a required diet for a diagnosed illness, allergy, or health problem
- Choosing to eat a restricted range of foods that are considered to be safe
- Unusual interest in the health of what others are eating
- Spending hours per day thinking about what food might be served at upcoming events
- Obsessive following of food and healthy lifestyle blogs on social media

One patient of mine who was gluten-free and vegan would allow herself a daily snack of 18 almonds that she would count out before leaving for work to eat for her 3 p.m. snack. She wouldn't eat in restaurants because of her fear that traces of unacceptable ingredients might be used. Her fear of eating something that she didn't consider okay was akin to that of someone who had potentially fatal food allergies. This kind of dietary control is only a more extreme version of the fear that many of my patients express about letting go of the strict rules governing their diets. For many, restrictive eating is a way to lessen concern about sudden weight gain. Orthorexia is further down the same continuum of using tight control to cope with the fear of the dreaded slippery slope: that the slightest relaxation of the rules will lead to a breakdown of their control over food, resulting in unimaginable weight gain.

Once again you can see how pervasive such binary reasoning can be in contributing to various forms of emotional eating. Such tight management of their diet reassures emotional eaters that if they can only exercise enough discipline, they'll maintain control of their eating; the alternative is chaos and potential disaster. The pattern of going from strict restriction to uncontrolled eating is essentially the same for those with orthorexic tendencies as for other repeat dieters, but the more extreme ritualistic behavior may present a greater challenge to letting go of the diet mentality.

Dieting Is Not the Answer

In the winter of 1944, World War II was ending and there were horrific stories of widespread starvation across Europe. The American government would soon be responsible for a massive refeeding project overseas, but there were no medical guidelines for how this should be done. Ancel Keys, a professor of physiology at the University of Minnesota, had been involved at the start of the war in the development of field rations for the American military. Now he was asked to design a study that could provide data to guide the refeeding project. Thirty-six men volunteered to participate in a year-long study of starvation. These men were all conscientious objectors who were allowed to participate in human performance studies as an alternative to military service.

During the first three months of the study, each participant was fed a tightly controlled diet intended to standardize his weight to match the average for American men of his height. Most needed to gain a fair amount. After the three-month standardization phase, during which the volunteers' three daily meals totaled about 3200 calories, the six-month starvation phase of the experiment began. To reproduce the effects of involuntary starvation, the men's calorie allotment was cut approximately in half. In a single day, the average number of calories allowed in the Minnesota experiment was 1570 per day.

To put this in context, a very low-calorie diet today would be about 1500 calories for a man and even less for a woman. So a contemporary weight-loss regimen would recommend fewer calories than an experiment intended to study starvation! This made me wonder about the restrictive diets of many people I treat in therapy. What are the psychological consequences of such a diet? How might it affect adherence when meals aren't being carefully controlled as they were in the experiment? After losing weight on such a diet does eating just return to normal? What are the effects of this kind of self-deprivation on the body's metabolism afterward?

In the starvation experiment, the psychological effects of the diet began quickly and soon became dramatic. After just a few weeks, volunteers who kept diaries began to describe how the time between meals had become difficult. One participant began to have nightmares about cannibalism—dreaming that he was the cannibal. This affected that volunteer's adherence to the routine as well. In an effort to end these dreams, he began cheating on the diet. During their unsupervised free time, he began to leave the university campus where the experiment was being held, to go into the nearby town where he would buy milkshakes and ice cream. The cheating was quickly discovered because his expected weight loss had leveled off. But even after he was caught and his freedom to leave campus was taken away, he found other ways to cheat on the diet and he was soon released from the experiment.

Although this was the earliest psychological reaction among the participants, the others soon began to show signs of abnormal food preoccupation as well. One notable incident occurred when Dr. Keys, the director of the experiment, decided to offer a relief meal to the group in order to boost morale and hopefully prevent others from cheating. The calorie content of this meal was considerably more generous than the typical ration, and it included an orange for dessert. When the men finished eating and they were ready to return their trays, nothing was left but the silverware, plates, used napkins, and orange peels. As Todd Tucker described the scene in his book, *The Great Starvation Experiment*, "None of them could bring themselves to throw it away. The idea came to them collectively. They picked up the orange peel and ate it, every one of them" (Tucker, 2006, p. 127). Keep in mind that this was after a relief meal of 2,366 calories, which followed fifteen weeks at the starvation level. The impulse to eat orange peels was not borne of hunger, but psychological scarcity.

As the days wore on, there were more incidents of cheating. Another person was dropped from the experiment when, alone at his night job in a grocery store in town, he suddenly found himself bingeing on stale cookies and rotten bananas that he was about to throw into the dumpster. Another had to fight the urge to root through a trashcan full of decaying garbage while on his daily walk.

Although the purpose of the experiment was to learn how to safely feed starving civilians, the volunteers' stories also highlight important lessons about the effects of dieting on the mind and body. The key lesson is that even restricting food to a degree that might be considered reasonable for a normal weight-loss diet, can have profound psychological and behavioral effects. It's worth taking that into account if you're thinking about starting a diet.

When I see patients for the first time, I always ask about their diet history and what their experience of dieting was like. A typical answer is, "The diet worked well. I lost a lot of weight on it!" Then I ask, "If it worked, why are you still having difficulty?" The most common response is, "I don't know. I just couldn't stick with it and gained all the weight back." In other words, they concluded that the diet was fine but they failed. I tell them it's the other way around. Yoni Freedhoff, a physician specializing in obesity medicine, puts it well: "Dieting has proven itself to be a tremendous failure over the years. But from all angles, we are taught to believe the opposite: that diets work, it's we who fail" (Freedhoff, 2014, p. 40).

Diets are likely to fail for a very simple reason: intentional dieting goes against how we evolved. Our bodies are well-prepared to resist weight loss. If you intend to lose more than about 5% of your current weight and maintain that over the long term, your body will do all it can to prevent it. Its only job is to keep you alive, and throughout human history, our main vulnerability has been starvation. Your body can only know how steady the food supply is by keeping track of how often and how much you eat. You may know that there's no danger, but your body doesn't.

When you're on a diet, the only reasonable interpretation that your body can come to is that you can't find enough calories, so it does what it's supposed to and helps you out by slowing everything down. You can try telling it, "No thanks, really, it's fine—I *want* to lose weight!" but your body just ignores you and continues to do its job. It's like the determined Boy Scout trying to help the elderly woman across the street while she's hitting him with her purse, insisting that she doesn't want to cross. You can protest all you want, but your body doesn't know or care that you really want to lose weight; it will do what it must to protect you from it.

Psychologist Traci Mann (2015), whose research focuses on self-control and dieting, lists three biological factors that make it virtually impossible to win the diet game: (1) neurological—your brain changes the way you perceive and think about food; (2) hormonal—the chemicals in your body that make you feel full decrease, and the ones that make you hungry increase; and (3) physiological—your metabolism slows down to conserve energy that would ordinarily be fueled by stored body fat. Like the Three-card Monte street hustle, the diet game may look easy as long as you're careful and pay attention, but no matter how closely you watch, the con man always wins.

For anyone who struggles with emotional eating, the best reason not to diet is that it will make the problem worse. However, if you stop trying to force your body to comply with your weight loss goal, you'll be in a better position to stop emotional eating and binge episodes permanently. By eating more regularly without depriving yourself, your body will recognize that food resources are readily available and you're in no danger of starvation. It will be less resistant to weight loss, which will allow you to lose the excess weight caused by emotional eating.

The more effort you put into suppressing your normal desire to eat, the more pressure you'll feel to binge. This effect has been documented in research conducted by psychologists Peter Herman and Janet Polivy (Herman & Polivy, 1980). In their studies, they compared dieters to nondieters by offering them a variety of food to eat without restrictions. The dieters, of course, were very careful about what they chose and how much they ate, and when they were allowed to eat freely, they consumed significantly less than the nondieters, as you would expect. Then the researchers made the same comparisons with one change: they had all participants drink a high-calorie milkshake and after that allowed them to eat as much as they wanted. Under this condition, the dieters consumed a great deal more than the nondieters.

In their review of these studies, the researchers concluded, "It seems that, for the dieters, the high-calorie forced load triggers the overeating by ruining the diet temporarily and unleashing the sort of lusty eating that is chronically restrained in the dieter" (Polivy & Herman, 1985, p. 195). It seems that when people are working hard to restrict what they eat, any violation of that effort can cause a release of the pent-up demand.

There are many areas of life that can be perceived as controlling, and any of them can increase the likelihood of triggering an episode of uncontrolled eating. But the perception that many foods must be restricted is the main source of control for almost all emotional eaters. Eventually, this feeling leads to a need to assert freedom from the experience of being controlled, and is expressed as defiant or rebellious eating. But this assertion of freedom isn't a true act of autonomous behavior so much as acting as if you're autonomous.

The Do-It-Yourself Autonomy Diet

So, what do you do if you really want to lose weight? Should you just give up hope of that ever happening? The answer is no; it is possible for a diet to work and to be sustainable over time.

There are many people who have lost a significant amount of weight and have kept it off permanently. These are not necessarily individuals who possess superhuman willpower; they're people whose motivation for change and the choices that they make comes from them alone. Greater social acceptance may be a welcome outcome, but it's not what motivates them. Their decision to make changes in their diet is based on their personal motives. The behaviors that they adopt are guided by their own common sense and preferences, rather than from diet books or online programs.

If losing weight was only a matter of having correct dietary information and following rules for eating well, then any standard commercial diet might be effective. But a diet must be more than nutritionally correct for it to work; it also has to work from the standpoint of human psychology. For a good example of a psychologically sound approach to dietary change, consider how vegetarians do it.

I'm sure you know many people who have chosen to adopt a vegetarian or vegan diet. I know many, but I've never heard of any who regularly lose control and binges on cheeseburgers. In spite of the fact that people who have given up eating meat have adopted significant restrictions in their diet and encounter some hardships to maintain it, they've chosen to do so for personal reasons, not because of perceived social pressure. A vegetarian may decide to give up meat for ethical, environmental, economic, or other reasons, but their motivation to do so is their own. Dieting for weight loss could work and be sustainable if your motivation is similar.

You may not be an expert in knowing how to create a healthy diet, but an effective alternative to traditional diets doesn't require expertise in any subject other than your own preferences, wants, and needs. Now, the only thing that you need to make the changes work is to apply that expertise to create your own version of a diet plan that's custom-tailored to fit you. It would look like normal eating: offering a wide variety of foods that you enjoy, and portions that are smaller but still satisfying to you. It may take some trial and error to figure out the choices and portion sizes that work best for you, but with common sense and the knowledge that you already have, you'll have plenty of opportunity to experiment.

"How Can I Know What I Really Want
If I Just Want to Eat Everything?"

It follows, then, that maintaining control over eating is not about willpower and self-restraint, it's about self-regulation—that is, using your judgment and practicing moderation rather than self-denial. When you view control as self-regulation instead of restraint, the question you can ask yourself when confronted with a decision about eating is not "Am I allowed to have it?" but "Do I want it and, if so, how much do I want?"

I imagine that your immediate response to that might be the same that I often hear from my patients: "That wouldn't work for me, because if I would allow myself to have any bad food, I'd end up eating everything!" Naturally, when you've had a history of restricting what you eat, and then periodically you lose control of your eating, you reasonably will conclude that the only thing holding you back is sheer restraint and willpower. So, you would wonder, how can I ever allow myself to have what I want?

This is where it's important to distinguish between wanting the food itself, versus wanting the freedom to have it. The former is typical of normal eating; the latter is characteristic of restrained eating. If you accept the idea that all foods are fine to eat, the only relevant question then is, "Do I really want it?" The two criteria you would use to answer that are whether it's something you generally enjoy eating, and, if so, whether now is a time that you would enjoy it. That would depend on your mood, appetite, alternative options, availability, and other factors. If the answer is yes, you would choose to take just enough to satisfy that desire. If it's something you like and you're in the mood to have it, that's all you really need to know.

But if you're a restrictive eater, any food that you regard as off-limits might as well be a scarce resource. That can cause an emotional craving for it even if you don't really want it. Think back to

Megan's experience in the restaurant. Her real preference was for the blackened redfish, but she had an opportunity—a special occasion that she believed would never come up again—to have the more indulgent lasagna that she didn't like as much. Her decision to have the lasagna allowed her to feel powerful, rebellious, free of dietary constraints, and in charge of her choices. Although soon after that she felt it was a failure of restraint and regretted it, at that moment she had taken control.

This sense of defiance and strength is a fleeting moment of satisfaction followed by remorse and anxiety. Defiance is only necessary if you believe you're being controlled by some powerful force outside of you. By changing your view of food's power over you, you accomplish for yourself what Toto did for Dorothy and her friends when he pulled the curtain aside to expose the Wizard of Oz. The Great and Powerful Pastry has much less power over you after you realize that it was you who gave it that power in the first place by being afraid of it. Once those foods are neutralized and powerless, it actually feels silly to rebel by eating them. The revolution is over, so what's the point?

If you know that you can have whatever you want, then your choice won't be influenced by other factors like the perception that you'll never get another chance to have it. The indulgent dessert that you're too full to enjoy right now will still be available when you're genuinely in the mood for it. Then, if you do want to have some, you can have as little a bite of it as it takes to satisfy the desire. If you want more, then you can eat a normal-sized portion and stop there because it's not the last time you'll ever have it again.

The important lesson to take away from this is that allowing yourself the freedom to have what you want when you want it makes it easier, not harder, to say no to what you don't want. In simpler terms, it will allow you to stop unwanted eating. In the following exercise, I'll use a fanciful scenario as a thought experiment that may allow you to get inside that mindset of self-regulated eating to understand how viewing all food as permitted and on the menu could work for you.

In this scenario, you can consider what the alternative to dieting would feel like. It would be a reality in which all foods are okay for you to eat, and they're all available. You can eat what you want so you don't have to fight the urge to eat. You also don't have to worry about missing out on an opportunity to have something. If you can overcome the feeling that a particular food is prohibited, then you can simply decide whether you want it or not. You would only think about whether you want to eat, what you want at that moment, and, if you do choose to have something, you would decide when you feel satisfied.

Imagine that all of your meals and snacks are available to you in unlimited quantities in a free buffet that's open 24 hours a day, 7 days a week. The buffet features high quality food of every variety imaginable. The table has only medium-sized plates and bowls, but you can refill them as often as you like. Of course, it may take some time to become accustomed to this gourmet version of an all-you-can-eat buffet, but once you get used to the idea, think about how you would make your selections for each meal.

Let's say you go for breakfast fairly early in the morning. If you wanted to, you could begin by grabbing a bowl and creating your favorite ice cream sundae with all the extras, but—think about it—would you? If not, consider what you would realistically choose. Some fruit? Sausage and eggs? A waffle with syrup? Maybe a simple bowl of cereal and milk?

Whatever you choose, you could go back for more when you've finished it, or choose something else that looks really good. What factors would you consider in deciding whether or not to have that tempting item? Let's say you're no longer hungry after your first plate of food but not yet really full. Would you go back for it then, or would you come back for it as a mid-morning snack? Do you consider the fact that the tempting item will still be there for breakfast the next day and you can have it then? Let's say you decide to wait for it. What would you do when the time came to return to the buffet? Would you reconsider how hungry you are, or would you have spent the morning thinking about it and go right back there? Remember, you'll be getting all of your meals and snacks whenever you want them, and they'll never run out of anything. Think about similar questions as they relate to lunch and dinner.

Now ask yourself whether in that scenario you would still be concerned that if you could eat anything, you'd eat everything. The only difference between that and real life is that in the real world you don't have access to a free gourmet smorgasbord that's open around the clock. But you can have whatever you choose to eat; the only question is, do you want it or not?

Exercise: Knowing the Difference Between Wanting to Eat and Wanting to Be Bad

On the next page is a chart (Table 2.1) that gives more specific guidance to distinguishing between the two types of wanting. When you look at the descriptions for each type, think about your own experience of wanting to eat for regular meals or snacks and for emotional eating episodes. The descriptions in the chart reflect both of those states of mind.

The goal of this exercise is to be able to have a better understanding of both types of experience: the normal desire to eat something versus wanting the opportunity to have something that you would ordinarily consider to be off-limits, but decide to eat it anyway. Consider what you're thinking before, during and after both of those types of experiences and try to think about how you can identify the differences between them in your own state of mind.

TABLE 2.1 – Distinguishing normal vs. emotional "want"

	Normal Eating "Want":	Emotional Eating "Want":
Motive	"I want to eat it;" for desire or appetite ("I'm in the mood for it"), it's about enjoying the food	"I can eat it;" defiant, transgressive ("I just want to be bad"), it's about wanting the opportunity before it's lost
Trigger	Hunger, in the mood, or time to eat	Feeling controlled, deprived, irritated
Attitude	Intentional, casual, untroubled	Impulsive, urgent, conflicted
Food choices	Varied, satisfying, enjoyable, desirable	Specific, indulgent, "forbidden" foods
Goal	To satisfy hunger and desire without overeating	To indulge, feel free, get relief from food obsession, "get it over with"
Thoughts while eating	Enjoyment, savoring of sensory qualities, mindful awareness	Shut off thoughts, mental autopilot, mindless eating
Stop cue	When satisfied without discomfort	When uncomfortably full
Feelings after eating	Gratified, sense of well-being	Guilt, remorse, need to recommit to diet

Restrained Eating and The Jack-in-the-Box Effect

In his 1863 essay "Winter Notes on Summer Impressions," Fyodor Dostoevsky wrote, "Try to pose for yourself this task: not to think of a polar bear, and you will see that the cursed thing will come to mind every minute." (Dostoevsky, 1955/2016, p. 69) This intuitive notion was tested in the 1980s, when psychologist Daniel Wegner and colleagues studied it and found that Dostoevsky's basic idea is partly correct, but the reality is more complex (Wegner, Schneider, Carter, & White, 1987). They tested it with two groups of psychology students who volunteered to participate in an experiment.

The participants in the first group were told to say whatever came to mind for 5 minutes while speaking into a tape recorder, but during that period they should try not to think of white bears. Then for the next 5-minute interval they were told to record all their thoughts, but this time they should try to think of white bears. The other group was given the same set of instructions for each of the two 5-minute periods, the only difference was that the instructions were given in the opposite order: during the first period they were asked to think about white bears, then to not think about them during the second session.

Wegner and colleagues found that neither group was able to completely suppress the white bear thoughts when asked to do so, but both groups made the effort and had similar success doing so. But when they were told to think about white bears, the group that was initially told to suppress the thoughts and then express them later had a rebound effect: they produced a surge of white bear thoughts that was much greater than the other participants who were initially instructed to allow the thoughts. This reminds me of how a jack-in-the-box is locked in until turning the crank unlocks the latch and it pops out with all of its suppressed energy.

This is a good way to understand the connection between dieting and emotional eating. The study by Herman and Polivy (1980) that I described earlier demonstrates exactly the same effect with restricted eating. The chronic dieters ate much more than normal eaters after all the participants in the study were given a milkshake to drink before eating from a buffet. This is the behavioral analogue of the white bear studies. They considered the shake to be a diet buster, and that was just enough to flip the on/off switch from "I'm on a diet" to "That's it, the diet's off so now I can eat anything!"

If there are certain foods that you want to avoid, you can try not to think about them. But every time you eat according to the diet, you have to be mindful of the foods that you're supposed to avoid. So ironically, they're on your mind all the time. Your effort to suppress any thought of them is like pushing down a jack-in-the-box until the top clicks shut. The lid will stay locked for a while as the crank gets turned, but only for a while, until you slip up and eat something that's not allowed on the diet and—surprise! The latch unlocks and the clown pops out full force.

Don't Micromanage Your Body

The upshot is that dieting is not sustainable. Diet programs offer false hope by producing short-term results. But in reality, the act of dieting has the opposite of your intended effect over the long term by making it more difficult to lose weight and easier to gain. Your body has an important say in the matter, and its view of dieting is very simple: like any food shortage, it's a threat to survival and it must be resisted.

In his classic book, *The Wisdom of the Body* (1932), the pioneering physiologist Walter Cannon coined the term *homeostasis* to describe how the body regulates itself and controls the various systems within it to maintain internal consistency. Blood pressure, blood chemistry, body temperature, enzyme activity, and so on, are all carefully coordinated and counterbalanced to maintain relatively constant levels.

With a healthy person, this process goes on independently, without needing any outside input. When you go for a checkup, it's the fine-tuned adjustments that your body makes in your various internal systems that tell your doctor that you're healthy when lab results are normal, and help her figure out what's wrong when they're not. One of the most complex of these systems is how the body regulates energy balance, which is how calories are converted into energy and either stored as fat or eliminated as solid waste, heat, or water. The body makes those executive decisions on a regular basis.

The metabolic system is designed to function on its own to maintain consistency. After eons of genetic mutations and the natural selection of those that work best, we've ended up with an intricate and complex design to regulate our energy intake and output. While the number of calories we take in may vary widely over days and weeks, our body is designed to maintain an almost unvarying weight. Yet many dieters apparently believe that it needs their close supervision and input in order to work well. When you diet, you're attempting to micromanage your body and override some of the crucial information that it uses to maintain the delicate balance of this complex system. It's like a corporate business manager asking a data scientist to step aside while he fixes an algorithm that's been working well.

FIGURE 2.1

Anything you do to try helping the process along is just one more burden that you're putting on your body to carry out a task that it's already doing amazingly well without your involvement. One example of this type of micromanagement is something I see very often. When someone eats a dessert after dinner or has some extra bread at brunch, they feel the need to work it off later that day at the gym or run an extra mile or two. Your body monitors what you eat and how much energy you burn, so your extra input is just more information that it has to sort out, which can be confusing and misleading. It may even try to compensate for the extra energy expenditure by conserving energy and storing more fat to avoid starvation. Just as important is the effect it has on your ability to eat normally and enjoy what you eat.

Studies done over the past 20 years that looked at the effects of dieting over the short- and long-term show that the body has a very robust mechanism to resist changes caused by cutting calories. The popular idea of "calories in/calories out" doesn't account for this. Instructions like "avoid oversized portions" and "eat fewer calories" are not wrong, but they are simplistic. They don't consider the complex interaction between the nutritional, physiological, and psychological forces that work together to determine body weight. When you diet, your body can't distinguish between voluntary self-deprivation and an actual food shortage, and it gets the message that there's not enough food out there. You may lose weight at first, but if over a period of time your body detects a pattern that there aren't enough calories, it will stop letting go of that stored energy. That's the plateau that dieters always hit when they stop losing weight even though they're staying on the diet regimen.

It seems reasonable to expect that the same would be true if you're getting enough total calories over a period of days or weeks, but you're eating at erratic intervals. To your body, that could mean that although there may not be a famine, it looks like the food supply is unpredictable or insecure. Your body would more likely err on the side of caution and be conservative about letting go of stored fat. On the other hand, if you're eating regularly and sufficiently, your body would be reassured that there's plenty of food available out there, and that it has nothing to worry about.

If your body could speak to you in plain English, here's what it might say a few weeks after you begin a new diet: "I'm not exactly sure what's going on, but there seems to have been some problems with the food supply over the past few weeks. But don't worry, I'm protecting you. I made all the necessary adjustments to make sure you'll still be getting enough calories to keep all the systems running so they won't be affected. Also, all that preoccupation about food that you've been experiencing? Yep, that's me. Just making sure you're sufficiently motivated to get enough to eat. So no worries—I've got your back!"

If you're on a very low-calorie diet, especially with increased exercise, after a few more weeks your overachieving body might report the following on its efforts to protect you: "Okay, so you may have noticed that you've lost some weight recently. That's because, unfortunately, I had to use some of the fat that I wisely put aside in our emergency reserve system when you were eating more than you needed to support your activity. But I also started rationing that emergency supply by slowing down your metabolic rate. So don't be alarmed if you notice that you're having a little more difficulty concentrating. That's because your brain uses up most of your energy. But don't worry—it's only a temporary brownout until the food supply gets replenished.

"You may also have noticed that your hair and nails are growing a bit more slowly than usual, so they may be a little dull and brittle for a while, but hey—bonus—you'll save money on haircuts and manicures! (Just kidding. I know it's hard.) Oh yeah, it's the same with your skin; it's flaky because, believe it or not, regenerating skin cells actually uses up energy too, and right now it's not essential. Try using more moisturizer.

"Don't thank me now. Save it for when the food crisis is over and you can put the weight back on to prepare for the next time this happens! I'll try to increase that emergency reserve too, just in case, because the food supply has been looking kind of iffy for a while now.

"Okay, got to get back to work."

The bottom line is that diets aren't merely ineffective, they're counterproductive. Most importantly, they're the main cause of emotional eating. Giving up dieting doesn't mean that you should give up any hope of losing weight. Emotional eating has the same effect as any overeating, and can increase your weight above the range that even your anxious body is comfortable with. Although I don't tell my patients that they should try to lose weight, it is typically an important consequence for them.

Fortunately, homeostasis once again comes to the rescue. Just as it regulates temperature and blood pressure, our bodies are naturally preset to settle within a certain weight range when we're eating normally. As with all genetic traits, that range differs among individuals. But if you're overweight, it's fair to assume that when you stop emotional eating, your body weight will return to whatever weight is normal for you without having to diet. However, I learned very early on, that once my patients make some progress and begin to lose weight, it often raises their expectations about weight loss. This required some modifications in my routine with my patients and the advice I give them about tracking their weight.

Checking in With the Scale

When I first began working with emotional eaters at a medically managed weight loss clinic, the staff followed the normal medical procedure of taking vitals, which included weighing the patient before each appointment. This routine was a carryover from when the program was a medical practice specializing in the management of obesity and weight loss. As they grew and added more dietitians and, later, psychologists, the practice of regular weigh-ins for all appointments continued among the nonmedical staff as well. The difference was that while the visits with the other health professionals were scheduled every month or two, the psychologists usually had weekly appointments, so patients had more frequent weigh-ins.

I soon began to notice that my patients seemed very anxious about weighing in. Before stepping on the scale, they would, of course, take their shoes off. But then sweaters, belts, and scarves came off as well. Those who had pockets would empty them of their keys, coins, and even hard candies before removing their watches and jewelry. I understood that they were anxious to see that they were making progress, but their focus and concern appeared to be more about the number on the scale than about the behavioral changes that they were working on to lose weight. Over time, they would usually lose weight, but from one week to the next progress was gradual and didn't always move in a continuous downward direction. Meanwhile, all the positive efforts my patients were making between sessions seemed less important to them than that number.

During the sessions, I would try to focus on how important their behavioral progress was toward achieving their goals and they would agree. But they continued to focus on the scale to see if their efforts were really having some impact. I became concerned that the weekly weigh-ins might have a negative impact on their motivation to continue making the changes they had begun if they felt that measurable progress wasn't happening quickly enough.

Then one day a patient came in for her appointment. She was smiling and sounded hopeful before the weigh-in because, as she put it, she "was really good" the previous week, and was looking forward to telling me all about it. But first, she was eager to get on the scale to see how much weight she had lost. When the number on the digital display settled, I could see her practically deflate. Not only did it fail to reflect her efforts, but she was actually two pounds higher than the previous week. Rather than telling me about the great food choices she made and the number of steps she recorded on her pedometer, she talked about how she felt like giving up. The entire session that week consisted of me trying to talk her out of quitting the program. Since that day, I have never weighed a patient.

After you have finished reading this book and, I hope, have resumed eating normally, you may still want to lose some weight. If you want a way to confirm that you're staying on track, and wonder if it's okay to use the scale for that purpose, I think it would be fine to check in as often as you like to monitor your weight. But if you're just starting to make progress changing your eating patterns, and you want to use the scale to see the impact that those changes are having on your weight, I would recommend that you hold off on weighing yourself for a while. First focus on your eating and the weight loss will follow. My concern is that you may feel like the patient I described who, despite her best efforts, still felt hopeless because the number on the scale didn't yet match her expectations.

When people begin a diet, they'll often say that they have a weight goal that they're trying to reach. I now consider a goal to be the expected result of any effort that you have complete control over. Behavior change is a goal. Weight loss is an outcome because it's affected by too many factors beyond your control. This distinction isn't just a matter of semantics. Confusing goals and outcomes is what leads people to wrongly blame themselves when their diets fail them.

Your Behavioral Scale

Weight loss happens eventually when you consistently make different choices than you did in the past. The scale only shows how quickly and to what degree your body is responding to those behaviors until it reaches its comfort zone. That may or may not be an accurate reflection of your efforts. But if your real goal is to make those choices and engage in those behaviors more consistently, then a more meaningful way to track your progress would be a measure that reflects those efforts directly.

I came up with a method to provide my patients with a simple way to track their daily, weekly and monthly progress toward their behavioral goals and keep score of their progress. The score that they get is directly tied to the frequency with which they engage in behaviors that they want to adopt. The solution I recommend is to use a calendar instead of the scale. This method of measurement is very simple: Identify three new behaviors that you want to work on. I usually recommend choosing one from each of three categories: eating, exercise, and lifestyle.

The first category would reflect changes that you make to actually reduce the amount of food that you normally eat. A typical example might be to experiment with taking portion sizes that are smaller than you're accustomed to by reducing your usual portion by half. Then, if you still want more, take the smallest extra portion that you think would be satisfying. Any other behavior that directly involves reducing how much you eat, without eliminating foods that you enjoy, would be appropriate choices for this category.

A second category could reflect lifestyle changes that relate to eating, but not directly to reducing intake; in fact, it might even involve eating when you normally wouldn't. An example of this is to eat three meals a day and add two small snacks between each of those meals. Another example is to eat at least one or two meals while sitting down at the table, preferably without distractions other than eating with others. Behaviors in this category tend to improve mindful eating and structure around meals.

A third category would involve increasing your level of activity from your current baseline. One example in this category is to identify activities that have easily measurable goals, like the number of steps you take each day using a pedometer or phone app. It doesn't matter if the activity is done at home, in a gym or around the neighborhood. It doesn't have to be objectively intense, as long as it is more than you're doing now. It should be something that you can measure, like the amount of time, number of steps or repetitions.

At the end of each day, write a number on the calendar that indicates how many of those behavioral goals you have accomplished that day (Figure 2.2). Each day's score will range from 0 to 3, and at the end of each week you can add up those numbers and track your progress. This new behavioral scale will have a weekly total between 0 and 21 and you can track the results over time. If you're hitting the maximum or close to it pretty regularly on any of those behaviors, that means you've reached that change goal, and you can replace the old behavioral goal with a different one. The important thing in choosing these behaviors is that at the end of the day, it should be clear whether you've done it or not.

FIGURE 2.2 – Tracking behavioral goals

SUNDAY	MONDAY	TUESDAY	WEDNESDAY	THURSDAY	FRIDAY	SATURDAY	Total
2	1	2	0	3	2	3	13

Now you'll have a meaningful goal and a number that you can keep track of that truly represents your efforts and progress. With the behavioral scale you control every aspect of it, and you should never be surprised by the results. You have the freedom to choose the behaviors and own the responsibility of reaching your goals.

Table 2.2 has some examples of the kind of changes that can have an effect, directly or indirectly, on weight loss. Fill in some of your own ideas below them. Using a wall calendar, write a number from 0 to 3 to record how many of those behavioral goals you have accomplished that day. You can total those amounts at the end of each week and track your progress over the course of each month. This will give you a score that offers meaningful feedback on your progress over time.

TABLE 2.2 – Examples of daily behavioral goals

Intake	Lifestyle	Activity
Cut usual portion sizes in half to start, add only as desired	Eat at least one meal sitting at the table	Reach daily goal for steps or distance
Use recommended portion on nutritional label to determine portion size	At least 3 daily servings of fruits or vegetable	Pushups or other strength exercise
Eliminate fast food meals, or limit to less than current frequency	Pack lunch from home instead of going out	Moderate exercise for 20–30 minutes a day

Shifting your focus from weight to behavior requires a corresponding change in attitude. While your emphasis on your behavior becomes more active, your approach to weight loss becomes more passive—in a good sense. Rather than anticipating the number on the scale with dread, you can observe it with interest. Your attitude about it should be similar to that of a scientist who is conducting an experiment with only one goal: getting clear data. It's an attitude of self-observation without judgment. As long as the scientist follows the procedures proposed for the experiment, she'll be in control of the process and there will be useful results. To do this involves adopting an attitude of curiosity about what those results will be rather than having a need to control what they should be.

When you apply this attitude to weight loss, you recognize that your behavior in the process is the only thing that you can directly control. Weight loss is simply the outcome of the choices you make when you adopt those behaviors. If you have excess weight to lose, and you make better choices consistently, weight loss will occur. How much you lose, and how quickly, however, is not predictable. That's why diet ads that promise that "you'll lose 30 pounds in 28 days" have disclaimers in the fine print, like "individual results may vary." No, results will *definitely* vary. The idea of aiming for a specific weight and a deadline to achieve it isn't setting a goal, it's setting an outcome, of which you have no direct control. If you focus instead on the behaviors that are necessary to reach that goal, the weight loss will follow.

KEY 3

BE STRATEGIC ABOUT CONTROL

The Many Meanings of Control

What do people mean when they say, "Control yourself"? When it comes to eating, it usually means "just say no" or "resist." In Key 2, I explained how self-doubt about food choices can make you want to look for outside advice to tell you how to gain more control over how you eat.

I encouraged you to trust your own intuition, which of course, is easy to say. I imagine that's like asking you to walk down a dimly-lit stairwell without using the handrails—and just trust your intuition. Even if you know exactly what to do, you would still feel pretty anxious about it. To feel ready to let go, you'll need to have confidence in your ability to take control of your eating without outside guidance.

When people think of applying self-control to their own behavior, they usually equate it with exerting self-restraint. This requires overriding or inhibiting their normal desires and impulses. This kind of control is exhibited by all four of the emotional eating types that I described in Key 1, each in different ways and not only in the realm of eating.

Emotional restraint is most apparent in the Suppressor, who clamps down tightly on any negative feelings, especially anger, because of her fear of what she might say if she expressed them.

The Appeaser also practices a form of self-restraint by being too accommodating in order to avoid a confrontation that might risk social rejection. She won't say no if someone asks her for a favor. This self-compelled compliance keeps her from expressing any resentment about being taken advantage of by others.

Imposters have to work much harder and more carefully to maintain what they believe is merely the appearance of competence. The Perfectionist has a similar challenge, since her need to be constantly vigilant to guard against making a mistake makes it impossible to let down her guard or relax her need to be in control. All the while, though, they're keeping tight control over revealing their fear of failure to anyone else, often even hiding it from themselves.

All of the four types share three traits that could make them reluctant to let go of control and act spontaneously: 1) the need to preserve an image that they believe others have of them, 2) the tendency toward all-or-nothing thinking, and 3) the pressure they put on themselves to comply with perceived social expectations. The result of these three tendencies result in their needing to maintain constant self-restraint, as if they're living their lives while holding their breath. This is consistent with the common view of self-control: to restrain or override one's instinctive or preferred behavior.

However, control can also have a very different meaning, one that we use all the time. The *Merriam-Webster's Collegiate Dictionary* defines control as follows: "To exercise restraining or directing influence over." Control not only implies restraining some action but also directing it. Whether it's a factory operator adjusting the speed of an assembly line, a golfer controlling the force and direction of his putter, or someone deciding what to eat and what size portion to take, all are forms of control that don't imply restraint. Similarly, we use terms like *quality control* and *climate control* to refer to a consistent regulated output. Yet none of these expressions of control refers to overriding or inhibiting a process.

It's clear that the idea of regulation and direction is an equally valid use of the word *control* when it comes to eating as well. Deciding whether you want to eat and, if so, what, when, and how much to eat, is all about maintaining control over your eating. In this sense, normal eating is about moderation through self-regulation, not self-restraint.

Other Uses of the Word Control

The word *control* is used in many other ways in regard to how we eat, and I'll be using the term often throughout the book. So before going further, I'll sort out the different ways the term is used and explain the significance of these distinctions. Consider this a glossary of control expressions. When you understand the kind of control that can be helpful to you in making your own food choices, you can reestablish your latent food intuition as a useful and trustworthy guide, and rely on it with confidence.

- *Out of control:* This is the sense that you don't have full command over your own behavior. It's as if some force inside you takes over and dictates how to behave. This is perhaps the single most distressing experience that people describe when they seek out help for emotional eating. This is especially so, since, as I illustrated in describing the four types of emotional eaters, they tend to place high value on maintaining that kind of control in most other areas of their lives.
- *External control:* The feeling that the decisions and choices that you make in your daily life are being determined, or at least influenced by, the perceived demands and judgments of others. This applies in particular to situations where it feels like unspecified social pressures to conform have such a strong influence on your desire to belong that they take priority over your own

wants and needs. External control tends to trigger a reaction to act in a contrary way, because by nature we feel the need to be in charge of our own lives. As I'll explain next in Key 4, this counterreaction is an attempt to assert autonomy, and is the motivation for emotional eating.

• *Autonomous control:* To be autonomous means having the capacity and freedom for self-governance, and it's the opposite of feeling externally controlled. It's a sense of self-determination that is essential in stopping unwanted behavior, and involves the attitude of self-confidence that I'm encouraging you to work toward. It's being free from the external pressure to lose weight and from being told how to eat. It's a state of mind that you can choose by reducing your focus on the need to please others and comply with their expectations in order to feel accepted by them. When you're autonomous, your choices and behavior reflect more accurately what you consider to be your true self.

• *Self-control:* As I explained above, *self-control* typically is thought of as holding back or overriding an impulse or desire. When such self-restraint is exercised as needed to maintain autonomous control, it's a part of healthy self-regulation. It's just like how applying the brakes when you need to stop your car is a necessary part of safe driving. You may want to get to your destination quickly, but you override that desire in the interest of safety. With eating, the key is that such restraint is balanced with the equivalent of using the accelerator when appropriate, as well. Self-denial is only a problem when it's applied automatically as a default to safeguard against the fear of losing control and being unable to moderate behavior.

I hope it's clear by now that applying control over your food choices through restraint and self-deprivation is almost never a successful diet strategy, nor a sensible approach to eating in general. Our minds are programmed to resist that kind of control and fight back against restrictions on our freedom, including self-imposed restrictions. If thinking of some foods as forbidden is negative control, then viewing all foods as being back on the menu and choosing what you want among permissible alternatives is positive control. This self-regulation or self-management is most effective for ending emotional eating and is sustainable over the long term.

People seem to like catchy names for different diet trends. These days, with so many people looking for a diet to follow, we might call what I'm describing "the mindful self-regulation diet." Our ancestors would call it "eating." But if you've struggled for years with making decisions about what and how to eat, it's not a simple thing. Understandably, you might want more concrete advice about how to make these decisions. I'll offer some suggestions for using positive control to help you make better choices around eating, without triggering the kind of negative feelings that usually come with dieting. These suggestions can be categorized as three areas of control around eating: hunger control, portion control, and mindful control.

Hunger Control: Stay Ahead of Your Appetite

The advice for people recovering from surgery is to "stay ahead of your pain." That means that patients should take their pain medication on a prescribed schedule instead of waiting until the pain becomes unbearable. Otherwise, it will be more difficult to control the pain, and when it becomes more intense, it becomes harder to control. This could result in repeatedly going from feeling extreme pain to being overmedicated, with both states being poorly managed.

The same problem applies to hunger. The longer you wait, the more likely it is that the discomfort will affect your judgment and you'll overestimate what you need. This isn't just an analogy; the hunger signal and the pain signal serve essentially the same purpose, which is to call attention to a potential problem that we may not otherwise be aware of. Just as someone can anticipate having pain for the first few days following surgery and take medication to prevent it, we can also anticipate that we'll start getting hungry about four hours after our last meal and eat something to prevent it. In both cases, the signal that something needs attention isn't necessary to make us aware of anything that we don't already know, and the alarm can be canceled before it's triggered.

Eating in anticipation of hunger is like paying your bills on time. If for no other reason, you pay on time because it's annoying to get a call from someone asking for payment. A better reason is that being late on your bills can lead to fees and dings on your credit—the financial equivalent of overeating when you wait to eat until you're hungry. Practically speaking, this means that anticipating the certainty of getting hungry every four hours or so. Developing the habit of eating three main meals and two snacks a day can help you keep your food choices and portion sizes smaller and more in tune with what satisfies you rather than simply responding to what you urgently need.

I encourage my patients to eat intuitively, and I know that the idea of eating before you get hungry contradicts what many other advocates of intuitive eating advise. I think the approach of intuitive eating is very helpful in that it encourages you to be more aware of your body's signals, like knowing when to stop eating and making food choices that are in tune with what you feel you want, which may also be what your body needs. In that and most other ways, it's the best way to reject the diet mentality and reclaim control of your eating. However, anticipating hunger before it starts can be an effective way to prevent that craving and discomfort from negatively influencing your food choices.

So why do we experience hunger in the first place if we're able to anticipate the need to eat without feeling hungry? An even more puzzling question is why do we get hungry every few hours, even though we can go for weeks without food? Throughout our evolutionary development, calories were scarce and difficult to obtain. It could take a great deal of effort to find enough food to prevent starvation. Although actual malnutrition could take much longer to have an effect on health, it might take only a day or two of hunger before a person would feel too weak to hunt. The adaptation of a very early hunger signal gave foragers a strong competitive advantage in obtaining scarce calories.

Portion Control: Know Your Size

The portion sizes that we put on our plates are a well-known contributor to the obesity epidemic of the past 25 years or so. This increase in portion sizes is primarily a problem of perception of need, and is easily influenced by what is considered normal. The United States Department of Agriculture has a website called Choose My Plate (https://www.choosemyplate.gov/), with a section called "Portion Distortion." It's intended to educate consumers about healthy portion sizes to counter these common misperceptions of what portions should look like. That distorted perception is formed mainly by what we see in advertisements, restaurants, and cafeterias. These are the places where we're most often exposed to professionally plated portions.

Casual dining and all-you-can-eat buffets offer large platters of inexpensive meals that entice consumers to get their money's worth. The buffets are profitable because the first items in a self-service buffet line are the least expensive and most filling foods and are loaded with carbs. By the time you get to the more expensive foods at the end of the line, your plate is full. The same is true of the large platters brought to the table by servers in restaurants. The overflowing items on these plates are usually French fries or pasta. This leads to a distorted image for many people of what a normal portion of potatoes, pasta, or other high-carb, high-calorie food would be, and that becomes the standard that influences how people eat at home. When people can no longer rely on their own judgment to guide how much they should put on their plates, they rely instead on what's modeled by the professionals. In the case of the food industry, that's determined more by profit margins than nutritional concerns.

There is, however, another way of using the industry's self-interest to guide you in determining more reasonable portion sizes. Food manufacturers are required to show the calories per serving in the nutrition facts on their packaging. They also have to show what portion sizes they're using to estimate how many calories are in each serving, which is displayed in large print. Since they want to minimize the number of calories listed, they will describe more reasonable and accurate recommended portions. So, a serving of Ben & Jerry's New York Super Fudge Chunk ice cream would be a half cup, which is about one scoop and contains 300 calories. Of course, armed with that information you might decide that half a scoop would be plenty. A serving of Triscuits is listed as six crackers for a total of 120 calories. Is that what you would have considered a normal portion? Try following those guidelines and see if you're satisfied with those amounts. If not, you can always have more, but at least you'll be fully informed.

There's also a type of distortion called *unit bias*, which is to view one packaged item as a serving, even though the size of that one item can be enormous. Think about the size of a giant Milky Way candy bar. If you look at the package, it will say, appropriately, that it's two servings. The problem is that most people buying it would still probably consider it one serving, albeit a large one, unless they were making an effort to be mindful of how much they were eating. My best advice in that situation is to look for the smallest available size of that item instead of the value size. It may cost more per ounce, but less per unit, so you'll eat less. Once you've finished it, I doubt you'll wish there were more.

I've found that the best rule of thumb for decreasing portion sizes with meals at home is to imagine what you would normally put on your plate, and take half of that. If you still want more after you've finished what you took, you can always go back for seconds, but then take half of the amount of your first portion. I discovered this when my children were very young and we would get a large pizza for all five of us. When we ordered, we asked that it be cut into 16 slices instead of the usual eight, to accommodate the hands and appetites of small children . Normally, with an eight-slice pie, I would take two to start, knowing I could have a third if I still wanted more, but I usually didn't. Now, with the pie cut in 16ths, I still took two of the smaller slices to start (remember unit bias), then added a third if I wanted more—and I usually did. I realized that even with the extra serving, my typical portion of three smaller slices was only three-quarters of my normal portion, and I didn't want more than that. But if they were the usual large slices, I never would have left half a slice uneaten.

When you go shopping for shoes or clothes, you don't randomly try things on in the store. You know what size you are and you go straight for the clothes that are on those racks. You've made many more food choices in your life than clothing choices, so you must know how well your food portions will fit you at least as well. The only difference is that how much you want to eat at any meal varies with how hungry you are. But if you follow the advice in the previous section about not waiting until you're hungry to eat, that variable should stay as stable over time as your clothing size.

The amount of food people put on their plates is often based on habit and external cues rather than the amount they actually want. People tend to take more from a large bag of chips than a small one and are more likely to put more on a 12-inch dinner plate than a 9-inch one. Many dietitians recommend using a smaller plate whenever you can. As portion sizes have gotten larger, plate sizes have expanded to fit our changing habits. When I saw a set of china dishware that someone had in their family since the 1920s, I was sure the set was missing dinner plates; all I saw were various sizes of what I thought were dessert plates. That's when I learned how dishware has evolved over the years.

After you've eaten, it may take a while for your brain to catch up with your stomach before you realize that you've had enough. So if you feel that you want to eat more and you can still comfortably do so, wait about 10 minutes. Better yet, enjoy a little dessert instead and call it a meal.

Try to avoid snacking directly from the package. Even if you're having something like potato chips, unless it's a single-serve pack, take the amount you want out of the large pack and put it on a plate or napkin (remember, portion sizes listed under Nutrition Facts are a good guide). How do you change that kind of behavior? It starts, as does all behavior change, with being mindful.

Another type of mental habit that can be challenging to overcome is how people act on beliefs and ingrained messages that they grew up with. Membership in the "clean plate club" is a great example of this problem. Many people grew up being told that they couldn't leave the table until they finished everything on their plate. As adults, they continue to hold on to the idea that leaving food on the plate and scraping it off into the garbage is wasteful and wrong. Instead, think about it like this: if you've had a good meal and are no longer hungry, and then you eat whatever is left just to clean your plate, what do you think will happen to that food? It will go to waste just as surely as if you dumped it directly into the trash. The only difference is that it goes through you first. If you're really concerned about wasting food, consider saving it for leftovers and have it for lunch the next day. Or start a compost pile and use it to grow vegetables in your backyard. If that's not practical, at least stop making your body a human garbage disposal and take smaller portions to begin with. If you still have food left over, put it directly into the garbage; it will be going there either way.

When people lose sight of how much food they really want, they'll look for other cues to determine how much to take. For example, when restaurants upsell—offering larger portion sizes or even full entrees for the price of one, customers may order food based on what they believe are good economic decisions. Is it a good value to eat more just because you paid for it and it's available? Is it really a good value when fast-food chains offer a value meal with a larger burger, fries, and soft drink for just a little more? It may seem so, but if the extra food isn't what you wanted to begin with, then it's still not what you want when they offer more of it. It's like buying shoes that are several sizes too big for you because you're getting more leather for the same price.

Mindful Control: Be in the Moment

Mindfulness is a word that's used a lot, but people are often unsure what it really means. I think of mindfulness as conscious awareness of what you're doing while you're doing it. Aside from knowing what you're eating, mindful eating is also about really enjoying the process instead of worrying about losing control or making the wrong decisions. In order to achieve that kind of here-and-now focus, you should first make the kinds of choices described above: choosing when, what, and how much to eat. Once you have made those decisions, you'll be able to let go of the questions and focus on what you're eating. This, of course, is a description of what to aim for; it may not be a realistic expectation for every meal that you eat. But even when you're eating a bowl of oatmeal, you can still give some thought to appreciating the sensory experience.

Taking pleasure in eating can actually have a moderating effect on how much you eat. When you focus on the quality of the meal, you need less of it to feel satisfied. As nutrition scientist Barbara Rolls writes, "Satiation, the end of hunger, is affected not merely by your previous experience with the food and the visual cues you get about its size, but by . . . smelling, chewing, and tasting the food; even the act of swallowing is important. These sensory experiences . . . play a role in satiety" (Rolls & Barnett, 1999, p. 278).

When I was finishing high school, just weeks from graduation, I was hospitalized with a severe intestinal inflammation. I ended up undergoing surgery and for a full week afterward, I was not allowed to have any food by mouth while I recovered. Instead, they inserted a nasogastric feeding tube to deliver all the nourishment I needed in a liquid formula that went directly into my stomach. That entire week, I never felt hungry and I was recovering quickly, so I was clearly well fed from a nutritional point of view. But one of the clearest memories I have from that time was watching TV from my hospital bed and waiting for the food commercials. I was far more interested in looking at the juicy burgers in those ads than the television shows that interrupted them. I craved every delicious morsel.

I realize now that my experience in the hospital wasn't very different from that of the men in the starvation experiment that I described at the beginning of Key 2. While I was far from starving, I was feeling a sensory deprivation that caused a similar psychological reaction. More than the food itself, I wanted the experience of chewing, tasting, and swallowing it. The only sensory experience I was able to enjoy was the visual pleasure of looking at food on TV, and watching while the people in the commercials ate.

Getting nutrients via special delivery that bypasses any sensory experience is not pleasurable; it's more like a job that just has to get done. Now, compare that to an experience you may have had eating at a really good restaurant. Many different elements came together to enhance your experience: the taste, texture, aroma, and presentation of the food, together with the ambience and the service, all combine to create a truly satisfying experience. Your anticipation of the meal was not about getting nutrition or feeling full.

In fact, if you had left the restaurant feeling stuffed, it would have actually taken away from your overall enjoyment.

Most of your daily experiences with food will likely fall somewhere between those two extremes of sensory deprivation and sensual indulgence. But when your goal is simply physical satisfaction from a meal, the cue to stop eating comes from only one sensory experience: the sense of fullness. When you eat with full awareness, you can also enjoy the food's texture, the pleasure of smell and taste, and the visual experience of color and presentation. The difference between these two approaches is not about the quality of the food itself, but the attention paid to it. That's mindful eating.

Mindful awareness is especially important while snacking on something like chips or popcorn that you know you could just continue mindlessly munching until there's nothing left. The irony in that situation is that this is when enjoyment is really the only point of eating, yet it's also when the tendency to just keep eating mechanically is most likely to be a problem. There is a way to think about the situation that not only can stop that from happening, but can enhance your enjoyment of the snack at the same time.

There is a concept in economics called diminishing marginal utility. It means that the utility—that is, the usefulness or the enjoyment of something—does not increase at the same rate with each additional unit of the item. It's the commonsense notion that an extra dollar is worth a lot less in satisfaction to people with very high incomes than to those with low incomes. By the same token, a piece of candy is worth more to someone who is on a diet than to someone who can eat whatever they want. Similarly, you experience less satisfaction with, say, the fifth spoonful of ice cream compared to the first. Even though each spoonful is identical, you get less pleasure from each additional one than you did from the one before.

In some situations, like eating, marginal utility is not only diminished, but can actually become negative. That is, at some point, the value to you of each added unit goes down. In other words, you really can have too much of a good thing. If you have experience with unwanted eating, that's exactly what happens. We have all had the experience of eating something that is enjoyable to a point, but after reaching that point, there's still more of it left. Think of a dish of cashew nuts or a box of chocolates, for example. You may have a real desire for a piece or two of whatever it is that you really enjoy, but if more is available, you're liable to continue eating far more than you need to satisfy that desire. Being mindfully aware of the enjoyment or pleasure that you experience from those first few pieces is an important way to prevent overeating them. It's especially important in avoiding the what-the-hell effect of going beyond some point that you feel crosses a line. That's often an opening to an episode of binge eating. The best way to illustrate this process is with a food-pleasure curve, as shown in Figure 3.1.

Imagine that you've just finished an enjoyable dinner and, of course, you're no longer hungry, but you'd like to end it with something sweet for dessert. There's a candy dish in front of you with eight individually wrapped Hershey's Kisses, which are about 25 calories each. You take one from the bowl. You unwrap it, pop it in your mouth and let it melt slowly so you can savor it. If you were to rate that pleasurable experience, you might give it a score of 7 on a scale from 1 to 10. You've achieved a high degree of anticipated pleasure for just 25 calories; an excellent return on a small caloric investment. So you decide to have a second one.

This time your pleasure goes up from 7 to 9, simply because you continue to enjoy it. This is an example of diminishing returns: since you've already had one, which took you from 0 to 7 on the scale, the added pleasure of another one is likely to bring it up only a few points more. Now you're at 50 calories and at 9 out of 10 on the pleasure scale, which is still a very nice return on investment. Let's assume that another one is not going to increase your enjoyment more than a fraction of a point now, but the experience was enjoyable, and you eat one more to prolong it. Now that you've satisfied your desire for chocolates, you can walk away from the table with a sweet memory added to your dining pleasure, knowing that you've reached the peak of enjoying those after-dinner candies.

This is where it can become a problem if you're not eating mindfully. Continuing the scenario, but instead of walking away happy, imagine that the bowl still has a handful of chocolates in it, and they're right there within easy reach. Out of habit, you keep eating them one by one until there are none left in the bowl. From this point forward, any feeling of regret that you have, whether it's imme-

FIGURE 3.1 – The negative utility of mindless eating

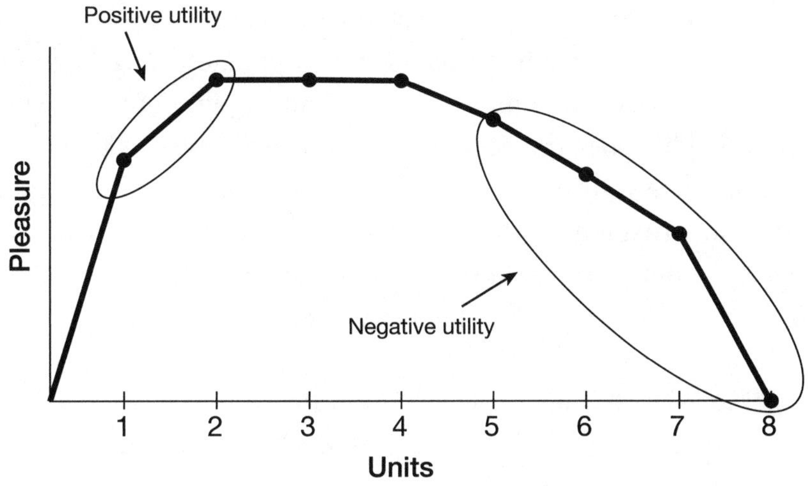

diate or delayed, will cancel out some or even all of the pleasure you initially experienced from the first three. Even though the fifth one tasted exactly the same as the first, which you fully enjoyed, your overall net experience results in less pleasure once you go beyond the fourth candy. This is an experience known as sensory fatigue. After repeated exposures to any sensory experience, positive or negative, you brain adjusts to the experience and becomes less sensitive to the repeated sensory stimulation. It's similar to how the brain develops tolerance to the effects of drugs in addiction. If you continue, you may consume a few hundred calories' worth of chocolate and walk away feeling worse than if you ate none at all.

It can be hard to be mindful in these situations. Our natural and mostly adaptive tendency is to tune out our routine behaviors, which allows us to focus on other tasks that require more attention. The problem is that this efficiency comes at a cost. The lack of attention can lead to behaviors that you regret, not because you're using poor judgment, but because you're not paying attention. If you're mindful of how much it would take to satisfy your hunger or desire for whatever you're eating, you can maximize your pleasure while keeping the amount you eat to a minimum.

At this point in reading this book, you probably have begun to think about food differently than you had thought about it when you started. If you're the person at the table with the bowl of chocolates, how has your thinking changed when you consider this scenario now? Imagine that the chocolate scenario occurred while you were still stuck in the pattern of emotional eating and think about how you would answer the following questions:

- Instead of having a few chocolates that you truly enjoy and then stopping, would you have allowed yourself to eat any at all? If not, why not?
- What would you have imagined would happen if you did eat just a few?
- Would you have been able to fully enjoy them without feeling anxious?
- If you resisted eating all or even just a few chocolates, would you have felt good about your ability to control the impulse?

- Would there have been a part of you that later on resented the fact that you resisted?

What, if anything, do your answers to the questions above tell you about how your thoughts about eating—especially eating just for enjoyment, as in the case of chocolates—have evolved to this point?

Engage the Senses

The best way to increase your mindful awareness of what you're eating is to focus on the various senses that you engage throughout the process. Imagine that you're a judge in a cooking or baking competition. You're not going to just chew and swallow large mouthfuls of whatever it is you're judging; you'll pay attention to all of the qualities of the food that engage your five senses. As chef and cooking scientist Kenji López-Alt explains, "Tasting is different from eating." Here's how he describes his approach to judging a pizza competition:

> I start by taking a slice from each pie with an across-pie-average of charring, bubbles, sauce, and cheese. I then bite just the tip, noting the pressure of the crust on my lower teeth to gauge its degree of crispness. As I pull the slice away from my mouth, applying just a bare soupçon of torque, I judge the effort it takes for the dough to tear. After carefully working my way up the side of each slice, I evaluate the cornicione (the raised rim of the pizza). (2015, pp. 26–27)

Imagine what a difference it would make if you used a similar approach to eating pizza at home. You would probably eat a lot less than you usually do, while enjoying it much more.

Mindfulness and the Art of Eating Chocolate

Of course, you don't have to judge everything you eat in order to eat mindfully, but the approach that López-Alt describes is a good example for how you can learn to engage your sensory experience of what you're eating. Here's an exercise that you can use to practice this approach. You will need one piece of chocolate, ideally a single square or a chocolate drop with a wrapper, like a Hershey's Kiss.

- Try to focus all of your attention on the chocolate. Approach the exercise with an open mind and a gentle curiosity.
- Pick up your wrapped chocolate, but don't unwrap it yet. Do you feel a sense of anticipation or an urge to immediately put the chocolate in your mouth?
- Place it in the palm of your hand and notice the shape. Feel the weight of it in your hand.
- Now begin to slowly open the wrapper. Look at the color and shape of the chocolate. Think about how you expect it will taste.
- Smell the chocolate. Does the smell trigger any other senses?
- Now slowly take a small bite of the chocolate, but do not chew it or swallow it. How does it feel as it melts in your mouth?
- Move the chocolate around in your mouth. Notice the taste and sensations of the chocolate on your tongue.
- Swallow the chocolate, focusing on the sensation.
- Is there a lingering taste?
- How do you feel physically and emotionally?
- How was this different from your general chocolate-eating experiences?

Another food that's frequently used to go through this exercise is a raisin. But I purposely chose an example that uses chocolate to demonstrate mindful eating. And just before this, I chose a description of how to taste a slice of pizza to demonstrate a food expert's approach to judging a cooking competition. You could probably guess what these two foods have in common: both are typically foods that are considered off-limits to people who struggle with emotional eating. Serial dieters in particular have an almost phobic response to these foods that can defy rational concerns about the food itself.

This fear isn't simply about their nutritional content or calorie density, because any concerns about that can be addressed by eating them in moderation. Rather it's that they're symbols of foods that are highly palatable and considered to be high-risk triggers for binge eating. But, as I hope you can recognize at this point, their status as prototypes of forbidden foods make that a self-fulfilling prediction. As long as these foods are off-limits on your diet, they're more likely to be first on your mind when you think about what you want to eat so taking them off the menu is sure to backfire.

Beyond the benefits of this exercise in helping you eat with more mindful awareness and enjoyment of food, it's also a demonstration of how all foods have a place in a healthy diet. If these foods aren't the ones that trigger you, there are probably many others that do. A good way to overcome that fear of these or any other forbidden foods is to eat them more mindfully, as in this exercise, so that you can enjoy them more while eating less.

UNDERSTAND THE MOTIVE

Pushing Back Against Control

When I ask my patients how they feel while they binge, they typically describe their experience as, at best, automatic, mechanical, and unenjoyable. In addition, they make the choice to binge even though they know, at least on some level, that they'll immediately regret it. The behavior makes them feel anxious about their loss of control, physically uncomfortable, and worried about the effect that these repeated episodes—which may occur several times a week and even daily—will have on their weight and health.

Considering the unpleasantness of this experience, we can dismiss the idea that people who binge eat are simply indulging a craving for tasty food. That belief more likely reflects the common experience that most people have had of making enjoyable but otherwise regrettable food choices, and they assume that binge eating is just an exaggerated version of that. But for my patients, as negative as their experience of emotional eating is overall, there is one aspect of it that offers something rewarding: at the moment they make the decision to let go of self-restraint—just before they act on it—they describe a surge of relief from the tension and preoccupation that they experienced while trying to resist the urge to binge.

My patients consistently describe some version of this internal conflict and the mixed feelings that go along with it. When they finally give in to it, it's as if the decision feels like the only way they can stop the noise of the battle going on in their head. The fact that they feel compelled to repeat the behavior despite all the negative effects they describe suggests that something is reinforcing it, and whatever it is must be very powerful. But what is it? My first clue about what might be driving the behavior came from one of the first patients I treated when I began working in the weight loss clinic. I'll call her Maria.

Maria was a successful and very driven sales manager who struggled with her weight. She had dieted on and off for most of her life and knew from experience that she wasn't able to stay on a diet for more than a few weeks. She came to the clinic hoping to lose weight and to stop dieting once and for all. I worked with her for several months, and between therapy, her own determination, and help from a dietitian, Maria had lost more than 15 pounds. By that time, she had been promoted to a management position in her company that required more travel, and she wasn't able to come in regularly for sessions. Although she had not yet reached her desired weight, she was happy with the progress she had made and felt that she could continue the work on her own.

About eight months after our last meeting, I received a call from Maria asking to resume our therapy sessions. Since we last met, she had gained back all the weight she had lost plus about six more pounds. She had occasionally binged in the past while on diets, but after she stopped therapy, those episodes became a regular occurrence, and she felt that her eating was getting completely out of control. When she returned to therapy, I asked how her new job was going. She said that she loved the challenges and responsibilities and was doing well. But she was traveling three to four days a week, and with a husband and two young children at home, she felt she no longer had control over her own life, especially in her personal and family relationships. When she was on the road, she ate mostly in restaurants with colleagues or clients. She was able to eat fairly normally when she was with others, but when she got back to her hotel room, she would eat from the snack bar and order room service. When she returned home from these trips, she would binge alone late at night in her kitchen, "just to let go." She didn't even enjoy the food she was eating beyond the first few bites and felt guilty and anxious afterward.

I was genuinely puzzled by the behavior that she was describing and asked her why she continued to eat like that if she wasn't enjoying it, and she said something that caught my attention: "Being able to eat without worrying about setting limits feels like taking a mini vacation or going to a spa whenever I want. Even though I'm not enjoying what I eat, it feels good to just let go of the rules." This made me think that perhaps letting go of control over eating might be a response in some way to feeling controlled by her new responsibilities and upset at their interference with her personal life.

Her comparison of binge eating to a vacation or spa helped me understand more clearly what reinforced the unwanted behavior. She felt overwhelmed by all the limits that her job was putting on her life, and the freedom to abandon the restraints of the diet was a key part of her motivation to binge. It wasn't simply being free from the diet restrictions; that was important, but she didn't have to go to the other extreme to do that. She could have gotten relief from those restrictions by simply quitting her diet and eating normally. By choosing to binge, though, she was actively taking back some sense of lost freedom and control of her life, even if only temporarily. That need was far stronger than the regret she knew she would feel later. This struck me as an important insight because it suggested that this bit of temporary freedom might be the reward that kept the behavior going. It also helped me to better understand something that another patient had told me a few weeks earlier.

Alex was an entrepreneur who owned a successful tech startup with hundreds of employees. He spent his workdays solving problems, but not the type of problems he had expected in his position. "I always thought I'd be spending most of my day making strategic decisions about how to grow my company. But now that it's successful, I find that I'm spending most of my time trying to solve everyone else's problems. It's just draining!"

Most evenings, after coming home to his spacious apartment where he lived alone, he would order a large pizza and chicken wings, put a beer and pile of snacks on a tray, and sit down in the den in front of his big-screen TV to watch sports. Although his doctor told him that he needed to lose weight, he described this evening ritual as a necessary indulgence to make up for spending the whole day taking care of everyone else's needs while ignoring his own. As he put it, "When I binge, it's like I'm saying, 'Now it's *me* time!'" He knew that this kind of "me time" was not what his doctor meant when he urged him to take care of himself, but he wasn't prepared to give up the routine.

Megan, who "just wanted to be bad," Maria, who wanted to "just let go of the rules," and Alex, who declared, "Now it's me time," were all telling me the same thing: the reason they binged was that it allowed them to push back against feeling controlled by others in order to regain a sense of personal autonomy. As they experienced it, the source of that control came mostly from work and relationships. But really, it came from themselves. In addition to whatever pressure others were putting on them, they were all high achievers who put pressure on themselves to succeed. They felt pressured by their own internal drive to compete, excel, and, for most, to diet.

Those whom I've treated for emotional eating are typically responding to pressure to lose weight, although it's usually the one area that they do not recognize as an outside source of control. Instead, they saw their need to diet as the obvious response to their emotional eating. From their point of view, it would seem reasonable that if you binge on a regular basis, you must be more careful about what you choose to eat. In their view, dieting is an effect, not a cause of emotional eating. They consider their problems with eating as an uncharacteristic failure of self-discipline on their part, and therefore especially frustrating. Although they may accept the goal of losing weight as desirable, they still feel controlled by it and use emotional eating as a response to feeling controlled.

Laissez les bons temps rouler!

When the demands of dieting combine with other sources of control, whether they're strains in personal relationships or crisis situations at work, the cumulative effect can trigger episodes of emotional eating. You may wonder how eating helps someone cope with all those other sources of control. After all, eating seems like an overly specific response that's unrelated to something like work or relationship stress. If you imagine trying to lift a large bucket loaded with many different heavy items, the strain of carrying it is caused by the overall weight, not by the type of items it contains. Being on a diet is only one layer in that bucket of demands, although a considerable one that you have to confront repeatedly each day.

Having to cope with all those different stressors can make you feel increasingly limited by forces beyond your control, and eventually the stress surpasses some personal threshold of what you can tolerate. Dieting may be only one of those stressors, but it's one whose rules and limitations may be violated in complete privacy, minimizing, at least temporarily, the inevitable sense of shame. Rebelling against that source of control makes the whole bucket lighter and a lot easier to carry around. That's one reason that emotional eating is so hard to stop.

The fact that different sources of stress can combine to reach that threshold of feeling controlled may account for why people attribute their emotional eating to such a wide range of causes. Since those other stressors are easy to identify as external causes, they also seem to be more plausible triggers of emotional eating than something like dieting, which seems to be more internally motivated.

When people break the rules, they feel they're taking back control. Ironically, most people experience breaking the diet rules as losing control, rather than taking it back. This is understandable, since all they're really aware of is a very helpless feeling, like driving on ice and going into an uncontrollable skid. You quickly realize that steering is useless, and all you can do is just wait until the car stops and hope for the best. As one patient told me, "When I decide to binge, it feels like I'm getting into a roller coaster just before it starts, thinking I don't want to do this. But once I'm locked in I just give up and go along for the ride."

Before I make the case that there's a basic human tendency to push back against control, I'll pose a challenge. Question: Aside from general drunken revelry and dissolute behavior, what do spring break, Mardi Gras, the twenty-first birthday bar crawl, and the bachelor party all have in common? Answer: Each is a type of ritual that marks either the start or conclusion of some type of limitation on people's freedom.

For many college students, spring break is more than just a chance to relax in the sun over vacation; it's a chance to let go of self-restraint and celebrate relief from the pressures of exams and papers. Other rituals mark the beginning rather than the end of a period of self-restraint; sort of a last fling of freedom. Mardi Gras immediately precedes the period of Lent, which has traditionally been marked by giving up some kind of pleasurable indulgence to prepare spiritually for Easter. However, rather than preparing for solemn reflection, Mardis Gras is celebrated in many cultures by abandoning inhibitions and overindulging. Of course, it has since moved far beyond its religious context and has become a chance for anyone to party. But the custom of letting go to mark the holiday has been around since the Middle Ages and even earlier, since Roman times, when pagan religions had similar springtime customs, perhaps in response to feeling closed in during the rainy winter months. Likewise, the bachelor party is often celebrated by close friends throwing a wild party to mark the end of the groom's (and often, the bride's) single lifestyle and impending commitment to monogamy. All of these rituals involve unrestrained behavior as a counterweight to the impending or recently concluded period of restraint.

Many people scheduled to undergo bariatric weight-loss surgery often binge a few days before the procedure as their way of marking what they incorrectly believe will be their last chance to eat normally. And recall that in the story about Megan changing her order in the restaurant from blackened redfish to lasagna, she was about to begin a diet the next day. The mind-set that underlies this reaction is the same that motivates the private behavior of emotional eating. In all of these situations, the behavior people engage in more often resembles a caricature of freedom rather than true autonomy. I call this pseudo-autonomy because it offers a momentary feeling of freedom that may scratch the itch to let go of self-restraint, but it's more like role-playing their fantasy of what real autonomy is like.

In all of these examples, there's some event that can be seen as a curtailment of personal freedom. Such events may be stressors of daily life that make you feel controlled, powerless, or trapped in some way that limits your ability to direct your own choices.

But the experiences that may trigger emotional eating often occur under the radar, unnoticed and misattributed to other causes. Recognizing these hidden triggers and how they connect to the unwanted behavior is a critical step in overcoming emotional eating.

Think about a situation that you consider to be a recurrent stressor. It may be your relationship with a boss or colleague at work, or an issue that comes up regularly between you and a significant other. You know the problem is there, but you don't want to confront it because it may just make things worse. One or more of those triggers can combine to make you look for other ways to break free.

Don't Think About Reverse Psychology

Marketers create slogans that appeal to our id—the part of us that wants to reject expectations and defy the rules. Ads will often describe their products as "sinfully delicious," "a guilty pleasure," or "a decadent indulgence." An ad for a hotel in Las Vegas has the tagline, "Just the right amount of wrong." There's even a menu item at a St. Louis custard stand called the Cardinal Sin Sundae. Advertising baits illustrate a basic feature of human nature: we're drawn to what we're told we can't (or feel we shouldn't) have. As police chief Wiggum on *The Simpsons* asked his son, "What *is* your fascination with my Forbidden Closet of Mystery?"[*]

Advertisers understand the effect that the opportunity to be bad, especially when the risk is low, has on consumers. The momentary sense of liberation that comes from breaking free of control

---

[*] The Simpsons, "This Little Wiggy" Season 9, Episode 18. Aired 3/22/98.

allows us to regain a sense of autonomy over how we conduct our lives. I refer to this as the transgressive motive because it drives us to engage in behavior that feels subversive. We do it in spite of the possible negative consequences or private guilt that may occur later, because the momentary feeling of freedom that it offers outweighs that cost.

One reason this happens is that when you're told to do something, it feels like a threat to your freedom, and you want to do the opposite to hold on to your ability to choose. This is known as *psychological reactance*. It describes the tendency of people to react against any outside control over their behavior. This perceived control is not limited to heavy-handed pressure; it can even be a simple suggestion that someone makes. The reaction is not a response to the merits of what the other person is suggesting, it's an instinctive reaction to any unsolicited influence that feels like a limitation on one's freedom.

Here's an example from my own recent experience. While driving home after picking up my wife at the airport, I was about to change lanes as we approached our exit. Just then, while we were talking about her trip, my wife reminded me that the exit was coming up. To be fair, she knows me well enough and had good reason to question whether I was paying full attention to the road while engaged in conversation. But this time her reminder was unnecessary, so I was a little annoyed. I said, "Thanks, sweetie— how did I ever manage while you were gone?" Then, instead of changing lanes right away as I had planned, I waited until the last moment. I don't think she even noticed my delayed response, but I did feel the need to prove, at least to myself, that I wasn't being controlled.

This may seem like a trivial incident, but that only emphasizes how common this kind of reaction is, even if it's often unnoticed. In fact, I only noticed it because I was working on this book at the time, so I was tuned in to such interactions. This is how you can begin to identify these triggers in your own life as well. Be aware of such small everyday incidents.

"The Spice of Perversity"

The human tendency to reject advice from others, and the often dire consequences, is found in the folklore of every culture. These stories endure because they reveal basic truths about human nature and teach us valuable lessons for our own lives. Mythology and literature are filled with examples of reactance. Odysseus risked the safety of his ship and crew when he defied Circe's warning to avoid the island of the Sirens; Pandora released all the evils of the world after she was warned not to open the mysterious container. And the familiar trope of forbidden desire being the ultimate aphrodisiac—from Amnon's lust for Tamar in the book of Samuel to Shakespeare's Romeo and Juliet—all demonstrate the human inclination to push back against the limits of authority.

A scene in Louisa May Alcott's *Little Women* illustrates reactance very clearly. Just as the oldest sister Meg seemed about to accept John Brooke's marriage proposal, she changed her mind because he seemed too confident that she would accept. Her Aunt March, described as someone who "possessed in perfection the art of rousing the spirit of opposition in the gentlest people" was unaware that Meg had just turned him down, and orders her not to marry him and threatens to disinherit her if she does. The narrator then notes:

> "The best of us have a spice of perversity in us, especially when we are young and in love. If Aunt March had begged Meg to accept John Brooke, she would probably have declared she couldn't think of it, but as she was preemptorily ordered not to like him, she immediately made up her mind that she would."

So, in response to her aunt's attempt to control her, Meg defiantly declares, "I shall marry whom I please, Aunt March, and you can leave your money to anyone you like!" (Alcott, 1868/2016, p. 124)

The archetypal tale of defiance and transgression is also the origin of the expression "forbidden fruit" and is perhaps the most appropriate example to represent the motive for emotional eating. In the Garden of Eden, Adam and Eve disobeyed the warning against eating the fruit of the Tree of Knowledge and, as punishment, were banished from Paradise. The moral that's usually drawn from this is that it's important to obey authority and control your impulse to give in to temptation.

However, as described in Genesis, the Garden of Eden was full of "every tree that was pleasant to the sight and good for food." Not only did the fruits of all the trees look equally tempting, but Adam was actually told to enjoy them all—well, all except *that* one. In fact, the only thing Adam and Eve knew about the fruit of the Tree of Knowledge was that they would die if they ate from it. Now, given all their options of tree fruits that were not only delicious but also safe to eat, how tempting could the fruit of that one forbidden tree have been?

In his book *Escape from Freedom*, psychologist Erich Fromm points out that how we judge the disobedience of Adam and Eve depends on one's perspective: "From the standpoint of the Church which represented authority, this is essentially sin; from the standpoint of man, however, this is the beginning of human freedom" (Fromm, 1941/1994). Fromm interprets the message of the Eden story in a way that's consistent with the concept of reactance: that an intrinsic part of human nature is to resist limits placed on our autonomy.

If you want to lose weight, and believe that eating demands discipline and control, it suggests that you feel there's some authority who is questioning your choices and dictating what to do. It may be another person, like a healthcare provider, family member, or fitness coach. More often, though, the authoritarian voice comes from within you—your superego, if you prefer. Our natural response is to defy this kind of control, and, in the process, we may even go against our own clear preferences.

If it seems strange to think of pressure that you put on yourself as external control, remember that perception is reality, and the need to diet can feel imposed. No one denies themselves the freedom to eat what they want because they enjoy feeling deprived or hungry; people diet only when they feel that they ought to do so. When you're offered dessert and you say, "I can't—I'm on a diet," your words reflect the sense that the source of control isn't you. You probably do want it, and you can choose to have it if you feel that it's okay to do so. The only reason you can't have it is because you feel that you're not allowed to eat dessert, not because you don't want to.

The Balance Scale

The sense of being controlled I heard in the stories of Megan, Maria, and Alex has since been echoed on a regular basis by almost all my other patients. I first began to hear this theme emerge as a pattern when they described their experiences prior to letting go of control. Once I recognized this pattern, I began listening for it when they describe their experience just before they binge. It wasn't difficult to find. I also didn't have to convince them of this connection by stretching or squeezing their story into the Procrustean bed of my theory to make the point. They recognized almost instantly the sense of emotional pressure that they were feeling just prior to an episode of binge eating.

This pressure is usually an experience that triggers weight concerns or the feeling that they have to carefully choose what they eat so they won't blow their calorie budget for the day. When it's not about weight or food, their thoughts are often about some conflict that they had at work or home where they felt powerless and controlled. Mostly, it was a combination of these, where a recent event on top of the pressure to diet pushed them over the threshold of how much freedom from control they could tolerate giving up.

I also noticed that their sense of urgency to binge and the amount they consumed seemed to correspond to the degree of outside pressure and demands that they were experiencing. The image of a simple balance scale came to mind (Figure 4.1). Picture a seesaw with a weight on each side, and each weight is close to the midpoint. One side of the seesaw represents the normal degree of external control that people experience and accept when they make reasonable accommodations to the needs of others. This side represents how people get along with each other as members of a social group. The other side corresponds to a reasonable degree of personal freedom or autonomy that all individuals need and expect. (I'll discuss this conflict between belonging and autonomy in more detail in Key 5.) The fact that the weights are near the middle denotes moderation on both sides.

However, when people experience outside pressure to conform as an unfair demand, it can make them feel unfairly controlled. If

FIGURE 4.1 – Balanced in moderation

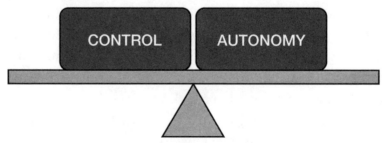

they comply anyway in order to feel accepted, the weight moves too far to the side of control and away from autonomy and tips the scale out of balance (Figure 4.2). This imbalance may be tolerated up to a point, especially for someone whose need to feel accepted by others is strong and wants to please them. Eventually, though, the imbalance becomes intolerable, and the person feels compelled to react by restoring equilibrium with an exaggerated display of autonomy.

FIGURE 4.2 – Unbalanced needs

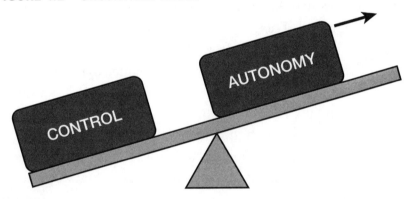

Dita had lost 15 pounds of pregnancy weight six months after giving birth. She was pleased about that, but she was upset that she still couldn't fit into her favorite jeans. She believed that wearing her jeans again would make her feel like she would fit right back in with her group of friends. Even though the diet she was on made her miserable, she believed that she just needed to lose a few more pounds, so she stayed on it. Eventually, though, she became increasingly irritated that the jeans still weren't fitting, and she binged out of frustration. Figure 4.3 illustrates Dita's experience and shows how her response to the pressure and frustration led to a transgressive response by emotional eating.

FIGURE 4.3 – Balanced at extremes

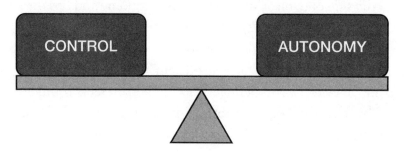

Many of my patients, especially the Appeaser types, may feel exploited by others but keep their resentment to themselves in order to get along. Then later, when they're alone, they binge to regain their sense of freedom from the pressure to conform—which is really their need to please—and restore balance to the scale. This is virtually always done privately, usually accompanied by a mix of resignation and angry defiance, like, "Aw, screw it!"

I realized that although the immediate goal for my patients was to restore that balance as quickly and easily as possible, it created a new problem. While the pressure and control they were feeling didn't go away, they now had to deal with the distress caused by emotional eating. It's no more effective than soaking one foot in scalding hot water and trying to balance the pain by placing the other foot in ice water. Trying to balance incompatible behaviors by offsetting them at opposite extremes doesn't result in moderation, it just adds a new problem.

Binge eating isn't a passive failure of self-restraint; it's a way to actively express that you still have the autonomy to make your own choices—even if they're bad ones. The fact that the food tastes good is not the attraction, it's a distraction from the fact that unrestrained eating is a misguided attempt to be free of the perceived control of dieting. And the temporary payoff is strong enough to reinforce the behavior, despite knowing that you'll feel worse later.

Jane Ogden, a professor of health psychology at the University of Surrey in England, came to the same conclusion in her research on emotional eating among dieters. Her experimental and interview data suggest that dieters experience an active reaction—or a "what the hell" effect—triggered in particular after eating a forbidden food, and respond with rebellious behavior and feelings of defiance (Ogden, 2010).

This new understanding of emotional eating means that the treatment of the disorder must be reconsidered. The traditional treatment approach to emotional eating is to focus only on the eating side of the scale. To oversimplify this approach for the sake of clarity, if the problem is that you have episodes of eating too much, the solution is to learn how to stop doing that. On the other hand, if the problem begins with feeling controlled, and emotional eating is a reaction to that, then the solution must involve reducing the subjective experience of being pressured.

Identifying Sources of Control

Trying to figure out the cause of emotional eating without understanding the relationship between autonomy and belonging is searching for the easy answer rather than a useful one, like the drunk looking under the lamppost late at night for the keys he lost in the alley. When he's asked why he's looking there if he lost them in the alley, he says, "Because this is where the light is!" There are countless sources of control in life. In addition to the compromises in autonomy that we make to live with other people, there are also ways that we feel controlled because of how we perceive a situation. As I'll explain in Key 6, many situations that we experience as controlling can be reevaluated and viewed differently. The truth is that even if you now understand where to look to discover what's causing your urge to binge, it may still be difficult to find. But at least you'll be looking in the right place.

The less controlled you feel, the less need you would have to react against it. The challenge, then, is to find a way to manage the pressures of life without feeling controlled by them. How do you respond to the pressures that we all experience, when they interfere with the autonomy that we all need? Is there a way to take owner-ship of these goals so you don't feel that the pressure to achieve them is being forced on you?

When you feel the impulse to binge, and you know that you don't really want to do it, asking yourself questions like the follow-ing may yield some useful insights:

- Am I feeling pressured at home or at work, or are there pres-sures that I impose on myself that have finally reached a tipping point?
- Am I feeling more controlled, defiant, or resistant to requests from others?
- Have I been struggling to hide my irritation or resentment about something that makes me angry?
- Has it been harder than usual for me to act graciously when I'm not feeling that way?
- As much as I want to lose weight, do I resent having to be on a diet?
- Have I been thinking a lot about what I can eat, or denying myself the occasional indulgences that other people seem to take for granted?

Exercises

The case examples presented earlier and the explanation in this chapter of what drives emotional eating leave some important take-away lessons to prevent repeated episodes of the behavior. Before going on to Key 5, think about and answer the following questions:

1. Identify something in your life that bothers you. If you felt free to say or do something about it, would that make a big difference in how you feel?
2. What do you imagine would be the worst outcome if you did say or do something about it?
3. Think of times in the past or present that an experience like that may have triggered an episode of unwanted eating. How did you feel when you knew you were going to eat or binge?

Thought Experiments

There are common events that most people can identify with that illustrate the ways we deal with the balance between autonomy and social belonging, and how that balance can tilt. Here are some thought experiments to help you understand those ideas from your own perspective. Write down your thoughts in response to the questions at the end of each. There are no right or wrong answers. The exercises are intended to highlight the daily situations in which we sacrifice autonomy, and to be more aware of how you may react to them.

Exercise 1

Imagine yourself as an adolescent sitting in your bedroom, when you look around and think, "This place is really a mess—I should clean it up." Just then, your mother pokes her head in the doorway, and says, "This room is a mess—please clean it up now!" What would you do, and more importantly, why?

_____

_____

_____

_____

_____

Exercise 2

Think about an incident in your own life, when someone in a position of authority or power told you what you should do, and instead you chose to do something different. What was the situation? Why did you make that choice? Was that what you really wanted, or were you feeling rebellious?

_____

_____

_____

_____

_____

Exercise 3

You're driving downtown and come to a red light. You probably feel okay about having to wait 60 seconds for the light to turn green. Now imagine that the driver in front of you is looking at his phone, and the light turns green. How would you feel then, and how long would it take before you lean on the horn? What's the difference?

_____

_____

_____

_____

_____

Exercise 4

Each of these senarios demonstrate how feeling unfairly controlled can provoke a desire to rebel or get angry. Can you come up with other examples from your own experiences?

_____

_____

_____

_____

_____

RESOLVE THE CONFLICT

Surrendering Autonomy

In Key 4, I described two sides of you that are in conflict. There's a conscious part that you think of as your real self. It's compliant, eager to please, and wants to do the right thing, including diet and exercise, and generally go along with social expectations. There's also a part that you're probably not aware of that's more rebellious. It instinctively reacts against restrictions on your freedom, including the freedom to choose what to eat. These are the two sides of the internal struggle that results in emotional eating, and this conflict must be understood in order to be resolved.

To understand the struggle, it's important to keep in mind that the rebellious self is not only a part of you, but it's actually an ally who, in its own way, is trying to act in your best interest. This side of you can make you feel angry when control feels excessive. It wants to help you stand up for yourself and protect your need to be autonomous. As I've explained, this is the side that can also goad you into unwanted eating.

It views dieting as a form of social control, and when you hit your limit of tolerating that, it encourages you to prove that you won't be pushed around. I've learned from my patients that emotional eating feels good in the moment when you're doing it not simply because it's tasty or because it soothes you when you're feeling down or stressed; both may be true, but they're secondary. The main reason is that it feels liberating to finally stand up for yourself. This part of you acts more out of an angry motive than a sad or depressed one. It's saying, "I'm mad as hell, and I'm not going to take it anymore!"

Yet, here's the paradox: in spite of the part of us that incites rebellion against limits on our freedom, we willingly give up freedom all the time. Whenever we accept a new job, get into a new relationship, or get a driver's license and agree to obey the rules of the road, we're voluntarily surrendering some degree of the autonomy that we had. If autonomy is so important to us, what's our incentive to do that?

The answer is that compliance with social norms is not a surrender; it's a trade-off. We accept control when we feel that the cost of compromising some autonomy is worth the benefits of making that sacrifice. The main benefit is the satisfaction of our need to belong and to feel accepted. Whether we're hoping to be accepted as full members in a well-ordered society or as a desirable partner in a meaningful personal relationship, the net balance of this trade-off is overwhelmingly positive.

The idea that we're always being pulled in two directions, trying to find a balance between our need for autonomy and our need for belonging, was originally proposed in 1941 by a psychiatrist named Andras Angyal, who saw the conflict between these two basic needs as a dynamic tension, "without [which] human behavior cannot be understood" (1941/1967, p. 173). One is a drive to govern our own lives and the other is our need to connect with others and be part of a greater whole. This "self-surrender," as he called it, allows us to satisfy the need for belonging while curbing unrestricted autonomy. Pressure to conform is powerful because it satisfies our need to belong and feel accepted.

Belonging is an essential part of being human. We're social

beings whose success has always depended on forging bonds with others. For our early human ancestors, survival could not be achieved solely through individual efforts. They survived fierce competition against rivals and adapted to the harshest conditions by maintaining strong communal ties as members of clans, villages, tribes, and religious groups. This required the creation of strong social bonds among group members that helped them to compete more effectively against other, less socially cooperative groups for scarce resources and territory (Wilson, 2015).

Maintaining strong ties required some compromise and sacrifice of individual needs in order to strengthen the group and ensure its viability. Altruistic behavior, like caring for others within the group—even beyond close family members—benefited all of the group members. Free-riders, or individual members who benefited from the group's resources but did not contribute in kind, would be shunned, isolated, or even permanently excluded—a virtual death sentence in premodern times.

Our need for others and our willingness to make personal sacrifices for them is still with us and causes us to seek acceptance in the modern version of tribal life, such as the political parties, religious groups, or sports teams that we support and the family and social networks to which we belong. The consequences of rejection may not be as dire today, but the need to belong and feel part of a larger whole is embedded in our minds and reflected in our behavior. We wait at red lights for traffic to clear, stand to the right on escalators and moving walkways to let others walk past us, and hold doors open for people who are entering behind us.

We may not benefit directly or instantly from these small acts of consideration, but cooperative behavior helps to ensure the smooth functioning of the society we live in and safeguards our place within it. On an individual level, we benefit by being seen as cooperators and not as free-riders or defectors. In these situations, accepting compromises to our autonomy allows us to earn a living, enjoy love and companionship, and drive around town safely without causing pileups at every intersection.

The idea of a fair trade-off helps us understand how society works and why we're willing to make sacrifices as members of it. It's understandable, that is, as long as it remains fair. But why do people make sacrifices that they know are unfair? Emotional eating occurs when people feel that they're giving up more than they're receiving. This is especially true of dieters who lose weight, yet don't experience the social acceptance that they had expected. It feels like there was no payoff for all the sacrifice and deprivation and it was a waste of effort. But this begs the question that I raised earlier: Why would anyone continue to make sacrifices like dieting to please others when they realize and feel resentful that their efforts are not rewarded? Why continue to surrender autonomy if the trade-off isn't fair?

One way to understand this is that some people may be more vulnerable to the need for acceptance or the threat of rejection than others. The example of Arlene, in the description of the Appeaser, illustrates how an imbalance between the two basic needs can lead to emotional eating. Arlene began to resent her friend's imposition on her free time, but she suppressed the urge to tell her how she felt to avoid risking rejection. Emotional eating allowed her to express her resentment by fighting back against the personal control that she imposed on herself, namely, her diet. In this way, she could act defiantly in private without risking social rejection.

Another reason that dieters' hope springs eternal is their tendency to blame themselves when the diet doesn't work. As I explain in Key 2, when a diet fails, most people place the blame on their own lack of commitment and motivation rather than their unrealistic expectation of dieting as an effective solution. "Maybe I just didn't stick with the diet long enough or follow it consistently. Next time, I'll just have to work harder." That pattern can repeat itself indefinitely as long as that belief persists.

If you consider the continuing popularity of diets since the mid-19th century, it would seem that dieters are not just willing but eager to sacrifice their freedom to eat what they want. If you think about it, though, it's not the diets themselves that are popular; it's the promises that the diet industry makes. You'll not only lose a lot of weight quickly, they tell us, but you can eat without feeling deprived, and you'll keep the weight off permanently. Apparently, people continue to believe this in spite of their own repeated experience that no diet can do those things.

What keeps hope alive and diet books popular is the belief that they just haven't found the right diet or that they didn't have enough willpower, but next time they will. They hold on to this hope because they believe that losing weight will make them more acceptable to others. But the reality is that they'll periodically feel the same resentment about that sacrifice that Arlene felt about her need to please others. That's when they'll feel an urge to rebel against that pressure and do exactly the opposite. When you think about it, that can sound a lot like "I just wanted to be bad."

Authority and Responsibility

Any task that has to get done requires the exercise of authority and responsibility. Authority is the power to determine what needs to get done and how to do it, while responsibility is the duty to carry it out. Ideally, both authority and responsibility for any task are held by the same person. That kind of control allows the person to have a stake in the outcome and to exercise autonomy in choosing how to do it, both of which improve the motivation to do the job well. When authority and responsibility are separate, as in economic systems with centralized control that give workers no authority to have input into the job that they're responsible for, they may do the job but have little motivation to do it well.

Dieters give up their authority over eating in two ways: first, by complying with the pressure they feel to lose weight, and then, if they do comply, by giving up at least some, and often complete, control over making decisions about what they eat. This is the type of split that can cause emotional eating: one side is responsible for making choices, without full authority over what to choose. It's true that they had the freedom to choose not to diet, but their experience of the pressure to comply makes it feel as if it wasn't truly an autonomous decision.

I observed this kind of conflict in my grandparents' relationship when I was young. In retrospect, I can now understand it better. My grandmother, Augusta, true to her name, was a formidable woman with a tendency to take control. When my grandfather, Joe, was told he had high blood pressure, his doctor recommended that he adopt a strict low-sodium diet to help bring it under control. I can only imagine that Gussie was with Joe at this appointment, taking notes while the doctor was making his recommendations. I knew for sure, though, that the kitchen was her domain, and she took it upon herself to make sure that his dietary restrictions were carried out to the letter.

Ordinarily, Joe would feel torn between his desire for salty snacks and concern for his health. If he was left alone to sort it out, he would have to weigh the short-term pleasure of potato chips against the long-term health risks. Of course, he might still make unhealthy choices, but knowing that the choice was entirely up to him, he would at least have to consider the risks. But once Gussie took over Joe's authority to monitor his intake, he was left with the only remaining side of the conflict: how to sneak those potato chips without getting caught. I'm sure he cared about his health, but Joe bristled under Gussie's control. While she did her best to watch everything he ate, she couldn't always be there. So occasionally, Joe would sneak some potato chips or a little herring on a saltine cracker.

Now, instead of this being a conflict between two different individuals, imagine how this same dynamic might play out between two sides of yourself. Ideally, the authority side persuades you to be mindful about your long-term well-being while the side that has the responsibility to choose is guided by your taste preferences. As long as the two sides work together, they balance each other's concerns, and you have the full authority and responsibility to make decisions so you can eat healthfully and happily. But if the authority side is more concerned about social pressure and weight loss, then, like Gussie, it will try to control your behavior and come down hard about how you ought to be more disciplined with your food decisions. The other side that's responsible for acting on those decisions still controls what you do and, since maintaining balance is necessary, may feel the need to react against that pressure.

When the culture is constantly sending the message to diet, about how to take care of yourself—what to eat and how much—it can feel like your freedom to make your own decisions is taken over by an outside source of control. To counterbalance that, you react against it. You may want to eat a salad, but if you feel that the *want to* is really more of an *ought to*, you're more likely to respond like Grandpa Joe and grab the dessert instead—whether you really want it or not.

How can understanding this internal struggle help you stop emotional eating? As with any dispute, internal conflicts can be negotiated. I'll explain how to do that even when both sides of the conflict are within you.

Negotiating with Yourself

One of the most helpful books that I've ever read in my development as a therapist wasn't assigned as part of my clinical training; in fact, it wasn't even intended as a guide for therapists. It was a business book called *Getting to Yes: Negotiating Agreement Without Giving In* (Fisher & Ury, 2011). The authors explain that in trying to resolve any disagreement, the most effective thing you can do is to find out what the other side wants. That means you must listen to, understand, and acknowledge the other person's point of view with curiosity and without judgment.

That can be more difficult than it sounds. The last thing that adversaries usually do is to try to really understand each other's arguments. Typically, their main goal is to make sure that their own argument gets heard. Really listening and trying to understand the position of someone who disagrees with you can feel like admitting defeat, as if you're giving credence to a position that you're trying to discredit while letting the other side just roll right over you. The reality, though, is that you don't actually yield an inch by listening to and understanding the other side's point of view from their perspective. Instead, it allows you to make clear that the differences are not based on a misunderstanding of their position. You understand it very well, and yet you still have a different view of the situation. When you allow others to state their position fully and then repeat it back in your own words, they're more likely to offer the same courtesy in return and listen carefully to your side of the argument.

I recognized the value of using this negotiating technique for therapy when I was working with couples and heard them talking over each other as they argued—not listening, but just waiting for the other to pause long enough to get a word in edgewise. Their voices got louder as they competed to be heard, and the conflict would spiral out of control. Instead of bridging the differences between them, this kind of fighting pushed them further apart. My intervention was to help them listen to each other and summarize their understanding of their partner's viewpoint as fairly as they could, without commentary or judgment, then ask their partner if the summary was accurate. After any corrections or additions, the other person would confirm that it reflected their view, and would then allow the first partner to explain their side of the argument.

This approach to resolving conflict works well for a number of reasons. On the most basic level, both parties clarify any potential misunderstandings about each other's position. The other person's view may not be what you assumed, and you may be closer to agreement than you thought. Another advantage to this approach is that listening carefully shows that you can respect the other person's viewpoint even if you don't agree with it which increases the chances for a resolution. The most important reason to use this is that understanding each other allows an opportunity to find some common ground, an ultimate destination that you both share and can agree to work toward together.

This last point is key to resolving internal conflict as well. It may not be a big leap of imagination to take a negotiating technique designed to resolve conflict between parties in business and diplomacy and apply it to help resolve interpersonal conflict between couples. But when I thought about the internal conflict that emotional eaters contend with, I wondered if patients might respond to the same intervention to resolve their own intrapersonal conflict. Of course, you can only negotiate with yourself if you can first see the two sides within you as if they were separate entities. According to some researchers, they effectively are.

In recent years, cognitive scientists have offered a theoretical explanation for this kind of internal conflict called *modularity of mind* (Kurzban, 2012; Pinker, 2009). The idea is that the mind consists of separate systems or modules that have specialized functions. These modules each have different goals or objectives with the ultimate purpose of helping us act in our own best interests. They usually work together toward that shared purpose, but since they're specialized, there may be circumstances that could cause different modules to have conflicting ideas of what our best interests are.

Let's say that one module is specialized to help us think about planning ahead. This evolutionary adaptation might have encouraged a hungry forager who finds a large patch of berries to ration how much he eats so he'll have enough food to last a while. At the same time, a different module may have evolved to encourage the same forager to take what he can get whenever he has the chance, and to eat the berries immediately. This would create the same internal conflict that you've probably felt about having a snack when it's available rather than waiting until you really want it.

Now think of what conflict might be going on when you wrestle with the urge to binge. To be able to overcome emotional eating, you must first understand how it's working for you. In this case, the module that creates the urge might be the one whose job it is to help you protect your autonomy. If your concern about social acceptance causes you to set aside your own needs in order to please others, this autonomy module may eventually react to protect you. This view of the tension between the need for autonomy versus the need for acceptance offers a different perspective on how to understand unwanted behaviors like emotional eating. Rather than viewing emotional eating as a failure of self-control, you can think of it instead as a way to resolve an internal conflict by restoring balance between those needs. Unfortunately, this results in behavior that's contrary to the needs of the other side, so instead of resolving the conflict, it escalates it.

To stop unwanted behavior, it's important to understand what you get out of engaging in it. There must be some benefit, and to stop the behavior you need to understand the payoff. Binge eating may not be wanted by the conscious part of you, but it is wanted by some part of you that you're not fully aware of. Listening to that side's point of view can help you understand how it's trying to be helpful. If you apply the approach to conflict resolution that I described, you can see that the struggle is between two legitimate needs that can be mutually exclusive. The side of you that works on belonging wants you to lose weight. The side that protects your autonomy rejects external pressures when it feels there's a threat to your freedom. But they both would prefer for you to just be happy and stay healthy without the constant turmoil caused by your conflict over dieting. That can only happen if you can help them negotiate a mutual understanding.

Relationship Therapy Within Yourself

Let's imagine that the two sides of you went to a therapist who specializes in treating couples, but this time the couple is the two modules within you that are at odds with each other. What would that session look like if it was played out? I imagine the side representing the long-term health module as an overly involved, concerned mother and the emotional eating side as her 16-year-old daughter who is a very good student and a little obsessive about her grades because she wants to get into a good college. Let's call them Mom and Kim.

Mom has become increasingly concerned about Kim because she has noticed that since the beginning of her junior year of high school, Kim has been occasionally bringing in fast-food meals and eating them in her room while she studies. She has also found some candy wrappers and empty snack bags in Kim's room and has noticed that Kim seems to be putting on some weight.

In the past, Mom had not felt the need to set any rules on junk food in the house, but in recent weeks, she has confronted Kim about her eating habits and has been monitoring more closely what she brings home. Finally, Mom told Kim that she will not allow her to bring any junk food into the house, and that she has to eat dinner with the rest of the family instead of ordering in or going out for fast food. Since those rules have been in force, Kim has been disregarding them and has been frequently going out for burgers and fries after school with her friends.

After a lot of arguments at home, they both agree to see a family therapist to sort it out. The therapist begins the first session by asking Kim for her perspective on what's going on between them. She admits that she has been disobeying her mother's new rules, but she feels that Mom is being too strict, and is treating her like a child. Kim says these restrictions make her want to eat out with her friends even more to show that she's old enough to make decisions about what she can do and can't be controlled like that by her mother. The therapist asks Kim if she understands her mother's concerns. She insists that her mother is just too controlling. But she acknowledges that she herself has had concerns about the way she's been eating and is unhappy that she's gaining weight.

The therapist turns to Mom for her thoughts. She responds that she's frankly surprised to hear Kim say that. Mom explains that from her perspective, Kim's behavior only confirmed to her that stricter rules were needed, and that without the restrictions Kim would have even more serious problems with eating. But she can understand how she may have made the problem worse by making Kim feel that she's being treated like a child and wants to rebel against her strict rules. After some discussion, they both agree with the therapist's suggestion that, for the next few weeks, Mom will stop monitoring what Kim is eating and Kim will commit to having dinner with the rest of the family whenever possible. As long as Mom stops commenting on her eating, Kim promises to make responsible food choices on her own.

The scene that I just described illustrates the kind of dialogue that you can conduct between your own internal modules. The parental module may be telling you that you must be stricter than other people about what you eat because you've had problems with controlling eating in the past. The adolescent module responds that if it weren't for such rigid diet restrictions, it would have no problem eating in a reasonably healthy way. Then, you can take the therapist's role and think about how to help the modules work out their differences. They may have different responsibilities but they have the same goal: to help improve your short-term and long-term well-being. Instead of acting like teammates who lose because they can't agree on a plan, they can see each other as partners who trust each other and win by working together.

That trust is crucial. For your parental side, especially, which has to begin by backing off from applying pressure to diet, it requires a leap of faith. It's hard to back off strict control and believe that it will lead to more responsible behavior, given past experience. On the other hand, the parental side's strategy of doubling down on restrictive eating has only led to the behavior getting worse, so the downside risk is low.

Exercise for Resolving the Internal Conflict

Think about the four types of emotional eaters that I described in Key 1. Choose one or two that you can identify with: the Appeaser, the Imposter, the Perfectionist, or the Suppressor, and describe it in terms of a conflict between the two sides as in the scenario above. You might think of them as parental-you versus adolescent-you or, perhaps, present-you versus future-you.

- Describe the conversation between the two sides of your internal conflict.
- How would present-you describe what it's like when she wants to eat something that future-you tells her that she shouldn't?
- How would you make the counterargument for future-you?
- Have each side explain her own point of view and how they might be able to compromise.

BOOST YOUR COPING SKILLS

Toughness Versus Strength

How would you define stress? Is it pressure to get something done? Is it an unusually heavy load of obligations that need to be met? Is it the need to meet a looming deadline? We may describe all of these experiences as stressful and feel that we understand the concept well enough. But being satisfied with this casual understanding can prevent us from thinking about what stress really means, what causes it, and how we can best cope with it.

The term *stress* is actually borrowed from the material sciences. It refers to what happens when pressure is applied to metal. When this happens, the material is stressed, which can affect its strength and resilience. Hans Selye was a Canadian endocrinologist who studied the biological effects of stress. He saw the same effect of psychological pressure on human health, and borrowed the term *stress* and applied it to psychological experiences that can also affect our strength, resilience, and ability to cope.

But we can take this analogy one step further to better understand how to cope more effectively with stress. In describing metals, there is a difference between toughness and strength. Toughness refers to a metal's ability to be compressed, pulled, or bent without breaking. It's a measure of the material's resilience. Strength, on the other hand, is a measure of how much force a metal can withstand before it bends. It describes the material's rigidity. Tough metals yield under stress, while strong metals withstand stress until they fracture and break. The same is true of people. Depending on how we cope, we can bend under pressure but stay intact, or we can try to be unyielding until we break.

Which is better, toughness or strength? For materials, it depends on what the metal is being used for. Tough metals, like gold and silver, are better for use in jewelry, where the piece is hammered, shaped and bent, while strong metals that resist the impact of external forces are preferred for construction. Similarly, some psychological coping strategies can be more useful than others, depending on the type of stress you're coping with.

Criticism and personal slights can be hurtful, but we can usually let them bounce off without leaving a mark. Coping with more difficult or ongoing life stressors, though, requires the resilience of tough metals. Strategies that allow us to bend without breaking can be most helpful to withstand events that can have a lasting impact on our lives. These experiences are unavoidable, so flexible coping allows us to bounce back from them. It's similar to the way large buildings in areas prone to earthquakes are constructed to sway with the ground shaking rather than resist it. The goal is to minimize damage from the event, not to eliminate it. The more quickly we can return to our normal lives, then the more stability we're able to experience over time. Later in this chapter, I'll describe the importance of acceptance and letting go, which is also important in dealing with loss.

Below I describe the three primary coping strategies that we use to manage stress: emotion-focused coping, problem-focused coping, and reappraisal. When you read the descriptions of each of these coping strategies, consider how effective each might be in addressing the type of stress that leads to emotional eating. In particular, think about the type of stress caused by two sources: the daily restraint and self-discipline to stay on a diet in the face of constant food choices and temptations, and the need to maintain balance between the offsetting needs of belonging and autonomy and how to cope with a significant imbalance between them.

Emotional Coping

Emotion-focused coping is an attempt to reverse the negative effects of stress. It's usually the first response that people choose among the three types of coping responses. It's the first choice not because it's the most effective, but because it's most instinctive. It's like a topical anesthetic for pain: it feels better in the moment, but it does nothing to fix the underlying problem, which will come back when the pain reliever wears off.

But when a problem is caused by something that won't go away with time, superficial and temporary measures can make the problem worse by delaying treatment. So it concerned me when a patient reported that a book she had read about emotional eating recommended calling a friend to chat when you feel the urge to binge. "How does that help?" she said. "And who *does* that?!" This and similar advice is simply not an effective tool. By not addressing the underlying issue, it can cause more problems than it solves.

When the pain is emotional, like when you're feeling stressed, depressed, or anxious, you'll also do what you can to feel better. Often, people try to manage their negative moods by counteracting them with pleasant experiences or at least by taking their focus away from the problem with self-distraction. Taking a warm, soothing bath, talking to a friend, going to a spa, and other forms of pleasurable self-indulgence are all common examples of emotion-focused coping. These aren't bad choices when the problem is temporary and will fade after some time. Then the best choice may be to have a pleasant distraction to take your mind off it.

Comfort eating and emotional eating are both forms of emotion-focused coping. The first is benign self-soothing behavior when the problem is temporary and all that's needed is some relief or distraction until the bad feelings pass. An example of a situation where emotional self-soothing would be reasonable might be a setback at work, like being told that a promised promotion won't happen as quickly as you had expected because of some unrelated situation that affects the timing. That's disappointing but not a career buster, and it's not personal. Instead of going out for drinks to celebrate with friends as you had planned, you may call in sick the next day to give yourself some time off before going back to work.

Emotional eating is also a form of emotion-focused coping, but the way it works is more complex. The positive feeling comes from a sense of liberation from restraint by breaking the rules of dieting. By offsetting the feeling of restriction or control, you experience a false feeling of autonomy, which offers some temporary relief. While comfort eating is a response to an occasional experience, emotional eating is a repeated response to an ongoing problem.

People use similar behaviors to defy external pressure, like procrastination, impulsive spending, binge drinking, road rage, shoplifting, risky sex, and drug use. As with emotional eating, these activities often begin as a way of seeking immediate relief from feeling stuck or restricted with limited solutions, but such behaviors can turn into severe problems when they involve serious risks and become the primary way to cope with stress.

Emotion-focused strategies for coping may be useful under circumstances like the following:

- When the problem, though distressing, is minor and not lasting, and you just need some relief or distraction to help you get past it.
- The problem only involves you, if you're not acting out against another person to deal with a hurtful response or disapproval from someone.

- The behavior that relieves stress doesn't create new problems, like turning into a habitual way of avoiding problems or shopping for things that you can't afford.

Problem-Solving Coping

If emotion-focused coping is meant to ameliorate the effects of stress, problem-focused coping works by solving the problem at its source. This strategy is the most direct and effective approach to reducing stress. It's available to use when a situation is clearly connected to the cause of the stress and is potentially solvable, even if the solution may not yet be obvious. Here's an example of how a patient of mine used problem-solving techniques to cope with a problem that was an ongoing trigger for her emotional eating.

Anna was a doctor working in a busy outpatient clinic, and she was very dedicated to giving her patients the best professional care that she could. However, in recent months, her patient schedule was constantly overbooked, and she began to feel that the practice was beginning to function more like a sweatshop than a medical clinic. This created a very stressful work situation and allowed her less time with her patients, and no time to take care of her own needs.

Despite her stress and time pressure, she still tried to give each of her patients the necessary time and full attention that they needed. But despite her best efforts, this added to the pressure that she was feeling and forced her to make compromises in her usual standard of care, which made her feel guilty and angry. When she came home, Anna was physically exhausted and emotionally spent, but she pushed herself to spend as much time as possible with her children before they went to bed. When it was time for her to eat something, she was in no mood to think about her diet. Instead of eating a reasonable dinner, she grazed on snack foods and leftovers from her children's plates while she cleaned up. Then, when her husband went to bed, she binged.

While discussing the situation in therapy, Anna said that she believed the clinic's administrators were only interested in increasing patient volume and revenue. I asked her how she knew that, and she acknowledged that her view of their motives was based on her assumptions rather than any evidence of their intentions. She set up a time to meet with the administrators to describe what she had been experiencing and clarify the reasons for the changes in the scheduling procedures.

Anna was surprised to learn that they had a very reasonable explanation for overbooking. The clinic had been getting too many last-minute cancellations and no-shows. As a result, many doctors had gaps in their schedules, which was frustrating for them, and it also caused patients to wait longer than necessary to schedule an appointment. To address this problem, the administrators began double- and even triple-booking each appointment slot for all the providers in the clinic. However, Anna knew that late cancellations and no-shows varied according to specialty areas and that her department had fewer missed appointments than the others.

When she explained this to the administrators, they understood immediately and changed the policy to apply only to those specialties that had higher cancellation rates. Because she addressed it directly with them, she was able to see that the problem of over-scheduling was a well-intended way of fixing a problem and not a way to increase profits at the expense of staff burnout and patient care.

This case example illustrates three important steps in the problem-solving approach to coping with a stressful situation:

1. Challenge your assumptions about the cause of the problem. If Anna didn't question her initial understanding of the problem, she wouldn't have considered the possibility of convincing admin-

istrators that they should change the policy. (I discuss challenging assumptions in Key 7.)

2. Examine the underlying causes of the problem. It's impossible to come up with a practical solution without knowing the relevant factors that may be causing it. At first, Anna only experienced the effect of double-booking appointment slots without understanding the rationale behind the policy. She could find a solution only after understanding why this policy was created.

3. Take a cooperative approach to finding a solution, not an adversarial one. The people you'll need to confront about the problem will be more receptive to a different point of view if they're not put on the defensive. By understanding the administrators' interests, Anna could acknowledge the validity of their concerns and join them as an ally to find a mutually acceptable way to address them.[*]

This approach is the best and most direct way to deal with problems that cause stress, so it should always be the first one to consider in situations in which you feel constrained by external pressures. If you apply the three points listed above, you may be surprised to find that there are ways to solve seemingly impossible problems that can otherwise end up controlling your life.

Unfortunately, though, most problems are not so readily solvable even when you take the time to understand them. That's the shortcoming of problem solving. Consider some common work situations that cause people to feel constrained, such as a micromanaging boss. You may not be able to move to a position elsewhere in the company, and you're even less likely to be able to move your boss somewhere else.

Of course, in such circumstances, you can always quit your job, but that can create even more stress than you're currently under, so

---

[*] This is also a good example of the approach to conflict resolution described in Key 5.

it often isn't a practical solution. In fact, many, if not most, problems associated with external pressure are caused by circumstances that we have no direct control over. However, the reality is that no matter how stuck you feel or how difficult it is to solve the problem, you always have control over how you look at a situation, and changing that can have a profound impact on the stress you experience.

Reappraisal

That leaves you with the next choice: cognitive reappraisal or reframing. This entails first recognizing and questioning your automatic assumptions about how you're perceiving events that cause distress, and then considering the possibility that there are other ways of looking at the situation that would eliminate or at least reduce the distress. In contrast to problem solving, the ability to reframe the way you think about a problem is always available to you and is limited only by your imagination and willingness to challenge and change your assumptions. In the words of the Greek philosopher Epictetus, "We cannot choose our external circumstances, but we can always choose how we respond to them."

As opposed to emotion-focused coping, reappraising or reframing a situation isn't just a temporary fix. You can think of it as an internal way of solving a problem that can't be solved by other means. Like problem solving, it can actually get at the source of the problem by changing how you perceive it. As Max Planck, the theoretical physicist who won the Nobel Prize in 1918, said, "When you change the way you look at things, the things you look at change." Although in context he was explaining a basic principle of quantum mechanics, this statement could just as easily be applied to the concept of cognitive reappraisal.

Most of our mental life happens automatically, which psychologist Daniel Kahneman (a more recent Nobel winner, in 2000, for economics) refers to as "fast thinking" in his book *Thinking Fast and Slow* (2011). Fast thinking is the way we think intuitively and automatically without much careful thought. It's a shortcut to decision making that's more efficient than a more analytical thinking process, which is slow and would prevent us from getting much done. Fast thinking also allows us to respond quickly to a potential threat. The downside is that it can lead us to make faulty assumptions because it relies to a great extent on emotional reasoning.

For example, if you hear a fire alarm, you may first worry about the danger you might be in. This is emotional reasoning, which is very adaptive in response to an emergency, and it causes some anxiety. But when you reconsider your initial reaction, you might realize that may be just a test or a false alarm, so you go to investigate. Switching in this way from fast thinking, (your concern about a fire) to this kind of slower, analytic thinking allows you to reinterpret the experience as nonthreatening. Although most situations that cause us to feel worried, angry, or depressed are not as simple as that example, the general process of reassessing your first reaction and considering other evidence is the same.

In her book, *The Upside of Stress* (2015), psychologist Kelly McGonigal writes about stress and its effect on health. She explains how recent research demonstrates that stress, which was always considered to be harmful to health, has been misunderstood. She mentions a study that looked at the effects of high stress levels on mortality. The researchers examined records of close to 30,000 people who reported their levels of stress in the previous year. The participants also reported whether they believe that stress has a harmful effect on health.

When the researchers linked those surveys to the public death records over the next eight-year period, they found that people who reported high stress levels had a 43% higher death rate—but only among those who believed that stress was harmful to their health. So, yes, stress can be very harmful to health, as we health psychologists, whose mission is to help people reduce the effects of stress on their lives, have long believed. But among those who reported high stress but did not view stress as harmful to their health, there was a lower risk of dying—even lower than among those reporting little stress.

When that higher mortality rate is projected to a national level, it translates into more than 20,000 Americans who died prematurely each year, not from stress, but from the belief that stress is bad for you. If changing how you think about stress can have that kind of effect on your health, imagine the potential effect of changing your negative perceptions about daily life events. Reframing how you look at negative circumstances that you find yourself in—whether they make you feel controlled, stuck, or trapped, and without good options to change the situation—can have an enormous effect on your well-being and your sense of having autonomy and control in life.

Reappraisal is probably the most useful coping mechanism that we have because, unlike problem solving, it can be used in nearly any stressful situation. And unlike emotional coping, it's not simply a distraction or temporary relief from immediate pain or emotional distress. If you can learn to do it, it can be the most effective way to pull yourself out of a negative frame of mind. Once you recognize that you're feeling controlled, the next step is to challenge that perception. Ask yourself, "Am I really being controlled or can I look at this situation differently?"

The following case examples will help give you a clearer picture of how reappraisal can work to change the way people view the situation that they're in.

Case Example: Maya

Maya was a patient of mine who was in her last semester of law school. She'd had a job at a prestigious law firm over the previous summer where she was very happy and well-liked. More importantly, they saw her as a high-potential candidate and encouraged her to apply for a job as an associate there after she finished law school.

That fall she applied and interviewed with the senior partners, who told her that she would hear from them within the next few months. She waited to hear from them, assuming they would respond quickly, but by March, they still hadn't contacted her about the job. She didn't want to call them because she was afraid of how that would be perceived, and everyone she asked for advice told her to just sit tight and wait.

Meanwhile, her history of emotional eating, which she struggled with for years as an adolescent and undergraduate, came back with full force. She said that she felt like her entire future was on hold and that she felt powerless and controlled by the situation.

When we discussed the problem, I asked her why she was waiting for them to respond instead of considering other firms who might hire her. In fact, she had gotten some other offers while she waited for this one. She said that they were a big-name firm, the people there knew and liked her, and she felt more comfortable going back to a familiar situation.

I agreed that those were great reasons, and that it was understandable she would want to wait to hear from them. On the other hand, many other firms in the city could potentially offer her the same thing, even though she was not as familiar with them. She agreed but felt that she would still rather wait a while longer before exploring other options.

"So, you're choosing to wait?" I asked.

"Yes—I really had my heart set on this firm," she replied.

I told her that certainly sounded like a reasonable choice, and despite the stress it was causing her, she must have felt that the trade-off was worthwhile.

"Absolutely!" she said at once.

Since she wasn't catching on to my subtle hint, I expressed it a bit more clearly: "So, you agree that this is your choice, and no one else is pressuring you to make it?"

This time she hesitated before responding, and I could see that it was dawning on her that she really was making a choice and that she was not nearly as powerless as she had felt. "I guess that's true. I mean, of course—it's *my* choice."

In fact, she was even able to see that their slow response was valuable information that she could use to reevaluate her view of them, and it allowed her to consider the cons of working there, not just the pros. Until we discussed it, Maya had been taking a passive stance about the job, waiting for their response and feeling powerless. That feeling changed as soon as she reframed what she was doing as her own choice and reclaimed her autonomy in a more constructive way.

Reappraisal calls for cognitive flexibility. It's like the tough metals that I mentioned in the beginning of this chapter. Although it doesn't prevent the negative feelings caused by the experience, it does provide a way to bend without breaking. To reassess a situation that feels controlling means taking a step back and gaining some perspective. Maya couldn't make this shift on her own because from the moment the law firm encouraged her to apply, she began to see the next step in her career as an associate only at this firm. She felt emotionally attached to this vision and couldn't see other ways of looking at it until I prompted her to think differently and take ownership of the situation. Eventually, she did get an interview with that firm. I don't recall if she ever got an offer from them, but I do know that her emotional eating stopped.

Anthony

Anthony is another patient who was able to use reappraisal to change the effects of a stressful experience. He's a director in a corporate department and was told by his supervisor that if he wanted to advance in the company, he would need to take some courses for certification in his field. The classes met at a nearby university after work, and the company paid for them.

After the first few classes, Anthony realized that he already knew the material being taught, and it was a major disruption in his life to take evening classes and then commute home to the far suburbs. But it was too late to drop the course without having to refund the money to the company, so he had to sit through the rest of the classes. In addition to feeling stuck in this situation, the classes ended too late for him to catch the earlier train home, so he had to wait almost an hour for the next train, which meant going to sleep late while still having to get to work early the next morning.

While he waited at the train station one night, he felt angry and trapped. All he could think of was wanting to buy fast food to eat until the train was scheduled to leave. Although he wasn't hungry, he felt that letting go with food was a way to feel less stuck. He was angry that he had to take this worthless course, that it was late at night, that he had to take a train home because Uber charged extra at that time, and that the class made him just miss the earlier train, so he was stuck waiting for the later one.

We talked about how else he could look at his predicament in a way that would give him options. He eventually realized that the cost of Uber might be high compared to other times, but under the circumstances, it was either that or waiting an hour for the next train, getting home late, feeling tired in the morning, and feeling resentful about the entire situation. The extra cost was certainly worth avoiding all of that, especially if he considered the cost in money and calories of all the fast food he was eating while he waited. Most importantly, the fact that he felt trapped and without options made him view binge eating as the only freedom he had. He realized that his lack of options was due more to his narrow perspective about the situation than the actual choices available. His all-or-nothing thinking prevented him from even considering an easy and relatively low-cost solution to the problem.

Reappraising the Struggle Instead of the Situation

There is another way to cope that I view as closely related to reappraisal, so I'm including it here rather than as a separate coping strategy. Like reappraisal, it also involves changing your perception, but rather than reappraising how you feel about the external situation so that you can feel differently about it, you reappraise your emotional reaction to it instead.

Chicago winters have a well-deserved reputation for being brutal. Many times, I've stood on the "L" platform waiting for a train in the dark after work, with the wind chill bringing the temperature well below zero, shivering against the cold with every muscle in my body tensed up like a tightly wound rope. One time, I thought to myself that I couldn't do anything about the cold, and shivering was a reflex that's beyond my control. But this muscle tension was bothering me more than anything else and didn't seem to serve any good purpose.

So, with no protection from the wind blowing hard off the lake and the temperature in the teens, I did some relaxation exercises while waiting for the train to arrive. It did nothing to raise the atmospheric temperature or stop the cold wind, but I began to feel better. In my mind, it even felt warmer. The point, of course, is that no matter how helpless you may feel about the situation that you're in, you can still change how you react to it, and that's often where you experience most of your misery.

If you see the temptation to binge as something that is so threatening that you have to be constantly on guard and fight it whenever it's about to appear, then of course it will be a constant threat. But if you recognize that the real threat is the anticipation and fear that it's causing, you can accept it without being afraid of it. That doesn't mean resigning yourself to a hopeless situation; it means willingly accepting the thoughts that preoccupy you without being afraid that those thoughts are going to overwhelm you and make you binge.

You can accept your negative experiences without trying to fight the uncomfortable feelings that accompany them, just as the muscle tension that I felt in the cold was not only not worth the effort, it was far more uncomfortable than the cold itself. Doing this can free you up to cope more effectively with situations you're in instead of engaging in ineffective efforts to avoid them that will make you feel worse afterward, like emotional eating.

The real problem you're dealing with is not the food that you want to eat but are afraid will cause you to gain weight; it's also not about the loss of control that you believe may suddenly take over and drive your behavior in a scary and reckless way; and it's not the thoughts about those things that preoccupy your mind until you have no choice but to give in to that control. The real problem is your constant struggle against all of those things. Think about it like this: the only thing that imbues those problems with any power is you. That means that even if you don't feel that you have the ability to change the situation or even how you perceive it, you don't have to keep generating the power that allows those things to make you feel miserable.

Of all the food beliefs you have, whether certain foods are good or bad, allowed or forbidden, diet friendly or binge triggers, the belief that you don't have the freedom to choose what you want to eat can be the source of a great deal of mental preoccupation and anxiety. Everything is on the menu; the only question is: What do you want to eat? Not what you are allowed to eat or what you should eat. When you've had enough of whatever it is you choose, then any more than that is, literally, unwanted eating, so you would probably want to stop.

The way you interpret a situation can affect your experience of it and that, in turn, can influence how you respond to it. But that interpretation is biased in ways that you're not even aware of. We have a characteristic way of processing how we see things, so we're predisposed to jump to certain automatic conclusions. I'll explain that in Key 7.

If you like to journal and want to use a template for future situations that you may experience, consider a format like Figure 6.1. You can add to or change the column headings, but the one that allows you to change how you feel is, in more ways than one, the key.

FIGURE 6.1 – Journal template

Situation	First thoughts	What happens	"Key" to rethink it

CUE YOUR REASONING

Thinking Makes it So

In Key 6, I described the value of cognitive reappraisal as a coping strategy. In Key 7, I focus more closely on how that technique works, especially how changing your perception of what you experience as control can help in your efforts to end emotional eating. Later in this chapter, I'll discuss in more detail a type of thought distortion that I described briefly in Key 1 as nearly universal among emotional eaters, which is binary thinking, or thinking in all-or-nothing extremes.

In the second act of Shakespeare's *Hamlet,* the prince of Denmark welcomes his friends Rosencrantz and Guildenstern to his country. Hamlet greets them warmly and then sarcastically asks what they did to deserve being sent to "prison." Confused by his question, they ask what he means by that. Hamlet responds, "Denmark's a prison." They quibble over what makes a place feel like a prison, until one of them finally says, "We think not, my lord." Then Shakespeare makes a profound observation that concisely summarizes modern cognitive psychology: Hamlet concedes, "Why, then 'tis none to you; for there is nothing either good or bad but thinking makes it so. To me it is a prison."

Any unwanted response, either emotional or behavioral, is initiated by a thought. The mental process that leads from an initial experience that's interpreted as controlling to the behavioral response is automatic and unconscious. Reappraisal is a way to stop the process by slowing it down and challenging any link in that chain. When applied to emotional eating, the progression from experience to response can be summarized in a single sentence: Unwanted eating is a behavior caused by an emotional response to experiences that are interpreted as controlling.

I'll unpack this statement into a four-part sequence (Figure 7.1) with an explanation of each step in the process:

1. The *experience* of diet pressure: Since you were young, you've experienced a lot of pressure to diet, either directly or through the subtle and overt messages that are pervasive in our culture.

2. The *interpretation* of that as controlling: You internalize these messages and interpret them to mean that you may be less acceptable to others because you're not thin enough. To avoid rejection, you believe that you have no choice but to accept this sacrifice and decide to diet, although you're still unsure that this strategy will work.

3. The *emotional response* to the experience of being controlled: Over time, you resent the fact that you have to diet while others don't. You feel impatient and resentful when your sacrifice doesn't seem to pay off in weight loss or feeling more socially included. The foods that you felt you had been deprived of seem more desirable now than ever before.

4. The *behavioral response* of rejecting diet control with defiant eating: When you experience some other stress in any area of your life because you feel pressured to do something that you don't want to do, that feeling merges with your resentment about dieting, and you act on that feeling by rejecting the diet rules with emotional eating.

FIGURE 7.1

When we react in response to some experience, we're usually consciously aware only of the first and last of these four steps, the experience itself and the behavior, without necessarily understanding the connection between them, or any of the other steps for that matter. We usually don't need to think too much about this process, because we try to keep our minds relatively uncluttered so that we can manage all the other information that needs attention.

While most things that we experience aren't traumatic or stressful enough to require coping skills, unwanted behaviors like emotional eating can happen seemingly outside of your ability to do anything about it. That's when it's worthwhile to understand what goes on and pay more attention to the mental process that causes the behavior. If you're trying to deal more effectively with the stress of external control, you would need to know which of the steps give you the best opportunity to intervene and change what you experience.

When you break it all down, you'll see that it's the third step, the emotional response of feeling controlled, that leads directly to emotional eating. But the second step—the interpretation of the experience as controlling—is the weak link in this chain where mental filtering plays a role. Changing the interpretation can change the emotional response of feeling controlled, which breaks the link and prevents the unwanted behavior from occurring (Figure 7.2).

As I explained in Key 6 regarding problem-focused coping, if there is a possible solution to a problem in your situation, then

FIGURE 7.2

solving it would be the best approach to try first. If not, you would move on to the next step of this sequence, which is how you interpret the event. Your interpretation is shaped by how you filter experiences generally. Recognizing your go-to mental filter allows you to take a step back and think about how it may have helped shape your interpretation. This can allow you to better reframe your understanding of what happened.

The social pressure to lose weight is an undeniable reality. It's expressed in many overt and covert ways in our culture. But the mere fact that those messages are out there is not what causes that response. If you slow down the process between getting the message and reacting to it, and think about Hamlet's observation, that "thinking makes it so," you can see that good and bad, or any other black-and-white contrast, is a product of how you interpret such experiences. Reconsidering that interpretation will allow you to respond differently to that pressure. Conformity or defiance, dieting or overindulging are not the only options. You'll find that the most direct way to change the feeling of being controlled by social pressure is to first recognize that how you think about it is a choice that you can make.

It follows, then, that you could identify any circumstance in which you were feeling controlled, and think about it in a way that makes it feel less controlling. Alternatively, the same process of reinterpretation can allow you to view yourself differently too: as someone who has a greater degree of control and autonomy over her life than she thought. You can choose not to conform to the pressure. Either way, you would be able to reduce that sense of being stuck without options, which alone may be enough to avoid acting on the impulse to rebel. After all, the rebellion is over; you won.

When you become more aware that you have options of how to think, your interpretation of what you experience becomes a choice that can affect how you feel. A popular internet meme taken from A. A. Milne's *The House at Pooh Corner* is a scene in which Pooh and Piglet are walking through the forest. Piglet, with his customary anxiety filter, ponders aloud:

"Supposing a tree fell down, Pooh, when we were underneath it?"
"Supposing it didn't," said Pooh after careful thought.
Piglet was comforted by this.

If there are two ways to view an experience, both of which are at least equally plausible, and one way makes you feel miserable while the other makes you feel good, which one would you choose?

New York Magazine used to run a regular humor competition. One year it asked readers to come up with the best response to the following prompt: "What I should have said, and what I did say." The winning entry was, "What I should have said: 'Oh, I'm sure he's just stuck in traffic.' What I did say: 'Maybe he's dead.'" Now instead of the original instruction, substitute "What I did think" with "How I could think," and it would be a good example of choosing how you experience an event. For example, you've been looking for a job for several months and getting discouraged about the process. "What I did think: 'I'm stuck in this situation and I'm never going to find a decent job.' How I could think: 'I gain valuable experience from every interview, and I'm better prepared each time.'"

Our perceptions are consistently colored by our own unique way of looking at the world. It's like when you're wearing sunglasses and you forget you have them on; your perceptions are still affected by the tinted lenses whether you're aware of it or not. The way we view the world is shaped not only by certain universal cognitive biases but also by our unique cognitive filters which are colored by life experiences. These filters are hard to recognize, since they're such a pervasive part of how we think and how we view the world.

If you're feeling the urge to binge, first recognize this process and break it down to see if you can identify an experience, whether at home, at work, or in some other personal interaction, that might be troubling to you. Think about how you might be filtering the experience in a way that makes you feel controlled, and consider how your mental filter may be determining that. The primary goal is to recognize how you're interpreting the situation as controlling, so you can challenge your intuitive reaction to the event. As Daniel Kahneman put it when discussing the limitations of our ability to change the cognitive biases that we all contend with, "You can't improve intuition . . . what you can do is 'cue' reasoning" (Yagoda, 2018). This means that your intuitive response is only a first draft of your experience and you're not stuck with it. You can examine it for flaws before acting on it.

Here's an example of someone who was aware of her feelings of being stuck and resentful about her circumstances, but was unable to recognize that they were connected with her emotional eating.

Angela

Angela is a woman in her late 30s who has struggled with her weight since she was in her early teens. Although she was overweight in adulthood, she was able to maintain it at what she felt was an acceptable level until recently. Then, over a period of several months, she gained 25 pounds and recognized that her considerable knowledge of diet and nutrition, gained from many years of experience trying to lose weight, was not helping her control her eating.

When she came to seek help, she described how she had been coping in recent months with difficult family events. Angela's parents were divorced when she was in her 20s, although their marriage had been troubled long before that. Her father was abusive to her two older brothers, who had been estranged from him for years. She was the only one who had contact with him, although she was resentful over his past behavior and felt no affection for him. Six months ago, her father was diagnosed with terminal cancer and had no one to care for him. Angela felt obligated to take over the job of bringing him to his treatments and other medical appointments, taking time off from work when necessary. It was during this time that her eating worsened and she began to gain weight.

Although she recognized that the burden of caregiving might be connected to her eating, she thought that it would have stopped after she adjusted to the routine. But she didn't see how it could still be causing her to overeat after almost six months. After discussing the difference between normal caregiving stress and a situation that also involves feeling trapped and resentful but still obligated, she said, "Now it makes sense, because if it was my mother I was taking care of in the same way, I would have felt completely different, and I wouldn't have reacted like that."

All-or-Nothing Thinking

It's been said that there are two kinds of people: those who believe there are two kinds of people and those who don't. Many people have a way of thinking that reflects a view of the world as either/or, all or nothing, black and white. This is often called binary thinking, in the same sense that computers operate on a binary system of ones and zeros—there are no in-between values.

Someone who thinks like that is apt to evaluate food as either good or bad, permitted or forbidden, and they consider the outcome of their efforts in any area of life, including dieting, as either a success or failure. Since there are rarely shades of gray in how they view things, most decisions and judgments they make tend to be burdened by an exaggerated sense of significance. One patient told me that she wanted a taste of her daughter's ice cream, but resisted, and later binged. When I suggested that if she wants some ice cream it doesn't have to be forbidden, she reacted with horror: "No! Ice cream is *always* forbidden for me, because I can't go around eating ice cream, cake, and candy all day!"

Binary thinking describes a way of looking at the world that reduces perceptions, judgments, and practical decisions into two opposing and mutually exclusive options. This way of thinking offers the illusion of certainty, predictability, and clarity. But this kind of thinking skews judgment and requires constant vigilance, effort, and self-restraint to achieve success and avoid failure. Since I began specializing in the treatment of emotional eating, I've been struck by how common binary thinking is among my patients. Here are some common examples of how it can be expressed in emotional eating:

- Good foods and bad foods
- Failure or success
- Fat or thin
- In control or out of control
- "If I don't have it now, I will never be able to eat this again"

This kind of thinking can bring you into conflict with the real world, where choices and decisions are not absolute and require intuition, judgment, and a willingness to let go of certainty. This tends to be difficult, since emotional eaters understandably don't trust their instincts about food decisions. The uncertainty that results from this causes a great deal of mental preoccupation, which one can only maintain it for so long before giving up and letting go of restraint.

For many emotional eaters who think in this binary way, it's very common to feel that once they've gone off their diet, even a little, they've failed it completely and will have to start all over again. Meanwhile, until they do restart it, they're technically not dieting, so they feel there's a window of opportunity that allows them to eat whatever and however much they want. It's a good example of how rigid rule-following backfires by allowing you to ignore your own common sense and judgment.

This kind of reaction is what psychologist and addiction researcher Alan Marlatt referred to as the "abstinence violation effect" (Marlatt & Witkiewitz, 2005). Marlatt was interested in finding ways to help people who are being treated for alcoholism to prevent relapse following treatment. He found that when people don't trust their ability to deal with a situation that might trigger the urge to drink, they believe that their only way to stay sober is to completely avoid alcohol and events associated with drinking. When abstinence becomes a substitute for learning how to cope with these situations, it's inevitable that a lapse of some sort is going to occur, resulting in a full relapse. Marlatt's conclusion is that learning how to cope is more helpful than avoidance and abstinence.

This is especially true with emotional eating since, unlike alcohol or other drugs, it's impossible to avoid food or stressful situations. Relying on strict dieting and abstaining from certain foods that you consider to be triggers in order to prevent future episodes of emotional eating is a poor substitute for learning the skills to cope with such situations. It's true that having the confidence in yourself to learn these coping skills requires a certain leap of faith in the beginning. But the learning process can begin only by ending reliance on self-denial and avoidance as your primary way of coping.

Using binary thinking to increase your sense of certainty about food decisions will backfire and make emotional eating even more likely. That's because it forces you to categorize everything into two groups, and they all go in one or the other. Food is either good or bad, and your behavior is either in control or out of control. If you define being in control as allowing yourself zero cookies, then eating just one automatically puts you in the only remaining category, which is out-of-control. Then there's no difference between a minor lapse and a full-blown binge because they're both in the same category, and so you may as well eat the entire package of cookies since you've already crossed that line (Figure 7.3).

FIGURE 7.3 – Binary thinking

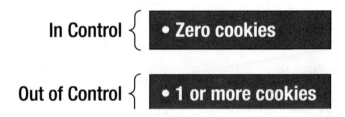

Binary thinking is a way to avoid making decisions about eating. The irony is that this is something that the binary extremes of dieting and binge eating have in common. If you just follow the diet and eat only what it tells you to eat, you don't have to make choices for yourself. By the same token, you also don't have to worry about making choices when you binge. They're two sides of the same coin. It's hard to say whether people think in this all or nothing way because they don't trust their judgment, or if they have difficult trusting their judgment because they're binary thinkers and food-related choices are not naturally either/or. Regardless of which comes first, though, it's important to challenge your black and white thinking and trust yourself to make reasonable decisions, even if they're imperfect.

The Scarcity Heuristic

Binary thinking can combine with another cognitive distortion that causes dieting to backfire. We use quick and dirty rules called heuristics to make judgments and solve problems. The fact that these heuristics are quick allows us to think more efficiently. But the fact that they're quick and dirty means they're not carefully thought through and lead to the type of thinking errors, or cognitive biases, that I referred to earlier. The scarcity heuristic is one that's especially relevant to emotional eating. It refers to our tendency to perceive things that are hard to obtain as more desirable.

Scarcity has that effect because it triggers our adaptive response to eat more of what we can find when the food supply is not secure. Dieting creates an artificial perception of scarcity, especially of tasty, caloric food, which is off-limits. This has the same effect as true scarcity on enhancing its desirability and makes the sense of urgency to eat it more intense. You believe that you'll start your diet over again the next day or after the weekend, and you tell yourself, "This time I'll be perfect and I'll never eat this stuff again, so I'll lose whatever weight I gain now anyway!"

This is the consequence of perfectionistic all-or-nothing thinking together with the diet mindset of the emotional eater. However, when all food is permissible, then the previously forbidden foods are suddenly more available, eliminating that false boost of desirability that comes from the perception that they're scarce.

Thought Experiment:
Changing Your Perception of Control

Now I'll offer a thought experiment that can help you experience more directly what reframing is like in a situation where you find yourself feeling controlled and frustrated by circumstances that you can't change. As you read this scenario, I'll offer some prompts to help you imagine how you might think, feel, and behave as you go through it.

Imagine that you have been commissioned to work on a writing project that may take weeks or more to finish. The sponsors of this project want to ensure that you have all the comfort and privacy necessary to allow you to focus on it, so they give you a very nicely furnished, fully-equipped apartment to work in. The apartment not only has a well-stocked kitchen and a high-end computer with fast internet, it has all the amenities you'll need to relax when you want to take a break, including a whirlpool bath, books, television, and music. You could easily stay there for several weeks or even longer without feeling bored or unproductive.

After you settle in, you explore the rooms, browse through the bookshelves, and then you decide to check out the hallway and the lounge area near the elevators. That's when you find out that the door is locked from the outside. You look around for a key but can't find one, so you decide that you don't really need to leave the apartment, and you have to get started on the work anyway.

- *To be continued, but pause here to consider:* What are your initial thoughts when you discover that the door is locked? How do you feel about discovering that you're locked in? What's your next step? Do you think about trying to get out, or trying to go back to work?

You decide to sit down at the desk and try working on the project, but you have difficulty concentrating. You keep thinking about the locked door and how you'll get out. It's not that you have to or even want to leave; you just want to know that you can. Until then, however, you feel trapped and you can't focus on anything else. While you struggle to focus on your work, you get up periodically to explore the contents of the apartment. During one of those breaks, you see a small drawer that you didn't notice before, and when you look inside, you find a key. You immediately try it on the door and it unlocks!

- *Consider:* What would you do? Would you open the door and go outside for a walk? Would you stay in, leaving the door unlocked? Would you lock it again, put the key back in the drawer, and go back to work?

You decide to return the key to the little drawer and go back to working on the project, but now you're able to concentrate without being distracted by thoughts of how or when you'll get out.

Now, consider this: regardless of what you choose to do after finding the key, everything in that room is exactly as it was before you found it. So what has happened that allowed you to go back and concentrate on the work even though your circumstances are the same as before? The only thing that has changed is your perception of being locked in. When you thought you couldn't get out, you couldn't work. But now you're in control and you have options.

This thought experiment demonstrates your ability to change a situation by perceiving it differently. When you're in a situation in which you feel stuck or controlled, if you can imagine other ways of looking at it, reframe how you perceive it or question the need to worry about it, then you have the tools to take control of how the situation affects you.

Now let's apply the same process to your thoughts and feelings in a situation that involves concerns about body image and weight.

Imagine that you're anticipating an upcoming event, like a reunion or wedding, where you'll be with good friends whom you haven't seen in several years. The event is two months away and you're feeling self-conscious about some extra weight that you've put on. You've already promised yourself that you'll never go on a diet again, because in the past you have always regained whatever weight you lost and felt very unhappy while you were dieting. On the other hand, you believe that if you can just lose about 5 pounds, you'll feel much better about going and less self-conscious about how you look.

First, think about how you would be feeling in the situation that I just described. Then read the questions below and as you do, be aware of how your thoughts and feelings might change. See if you can find the equivalent of the key in the drawer that might allow you to reappraise your circumstances.

- You're very aware of your own extra weight, but are your friends who will be there likely to be as aware of it as you are—if they notice anything at all?
- If they're not likely to be focused on your appearance while you're preoccupied with it, are you being fair to your friends (not to mention yourself) by allowing that to take your attention away from enjoying the time with them?
- If, in that situation, there was someone whom you cared about and were looking forward to seeing again who had put on a few pounds, would you think less of that person? If not, why do you think your friends would think less of you?
- Now ask yourself, if you wouldn't be judgmental of your friend who gained weight, could you be as kind and understanding to yourself as you would be toward her?

Now think about an actual situation that you're currently experiencing or have experienced in the past (perhaps it's the same as the scenario above) that made you feel similarly controlled or stuck. What were your initial thoughts that made you feel that way? How would you challenge those thoughts and think of a way that you can have a greater sense of control over your circumstances?

Exercise: Challenging Binary Thinking

For each binary choice below, write a word or a phrase that describes the middle ground between the extremes:

1. Good food/bad food _____
2. Binge/restrict _____
3. Ideal weight/overweight _____
4. In control/out of control _____
5. Healthy/unhealthy _____
6. Dietetic/fattening _____

All of these statements reflect binary thinking. For each item, choose whether you mostly agree or mostly disagree. If you mostly agree with any statement, restate it in a way that is not binary, as follows: Mostly agree, but . . . For example:

"If I eat even a little more than I think I should, I feel like I ruined my day."
Mostly agree, but I also realize that I don't have to be so rigid about the amount of food I eat at any meal. I can eat what I like and stop when I feel satisfied. Some days I may want to eat more than other days, and it all evens out over time.

1. I prefer choosing what to eat when the only options are my clear likes and dislikes.

   Mostly disagree

   Mostly agree, but I also realize that . . .

2. I am uncomfortable when I don't know all the ingredients of food that I'm offered.

   Mostly disagree

   Mostly agree, but I also realize that . . .

3. I prefer it when the rules for what I should and shouldn't eat are clear.

   Mostly disagree

   Mostly agree, but I also realize that . . .

4. I think all food can be divided into good or bad items.

   Mostly disagree

   Mostly agree, but I also realize that . . .

5. I'm uncomfortable not knowing what will be on the menu when I eat out.

   Mostly disagree

   Mostly agree, but I also realize that . . .

6. I want to clearly distinguish what foods are healthy for me to eat or not.

   Mostly disagree

   Mostly agree, but I also realize that . . .

7. Nutritional advice must be clearly true or false.

   Mostly disagree

   Mostly agree, but I also realize that . . .

8. I like to be sure I only eat foods that are nutritious for me.

   Mostly disagree

   Mostly agree, but I also realize that . . .

KEY 8

ACCEPT YOURSELF
AND THRIVE

In the previous chapters, I've made many different observations about what goes on in the process of developing and maintaining a pattern of emotional eating, why it's so difficult to end it, and how to overcome those difficulties. In this chapter, I review many of these points from the perspective of what I believe to be the most important factor in making and sustaining any kind of behavioral change over the long term: acceptance. This may sound somewhat paradoxical, since the whole point of wanting to change something about yourself is that you can't accept the status quo. The role of acceptance, though, is not that it's an end point, but rather, that it's a precondition for change. That idea should become clear as I explain in this chapter how acceptance is a necessary first step in the process. In the same way that a graduation ceremony is called a commencement, I'm ending the book by explaining how to begin the process of change.

The chapter is divided into four areas of acceptance: accepting yourself, accepting your own authority, accepting the change process, and accepting the urge. Each focuses on a different area of change, but all are based on the same idea: in order to move forward, you must first accept where you are now.

Accepting Yourself

When you struggle with eating, you're engaging in an ongoing conflict that tends to escalate. As explained in Key 5, the conflict is between two parts of you. One side tries to help you by taking on the role of the authority figure and says that you should diet. But that just provokes the other side that's trying to protect you from being controlled and resists the authority by saying, I'll do what I want to do, not what you say I ought to do. Every time you cycle through another round of this conflict between the two sides, you add another negative layer of experience in the struggle and become more entrenched in it. Trying to win those battles is like trying to free yourself from a Chinese finger trap: the more you try to pull out of it, the tighter it gets. The only way to get unstuck is to stop struggling, and ease out of the trap.

Compromise between the two sides of you is possible because they have the same goal: your well-being. One side tries to help by encouraging you to comply with social pressure, while the other side is trying to help you protect your autonomy. But since they both end up reacting to each other, their responses escalate, and your well-being—the very thing both sides have an interest in preserving—is at stake. When you understand what's going on internally, you can shift the battleground away from eating or avoiding this food or that, and accept the advice that both sides could agree on: eat what you want, but only what you want.

After you've read and practiced the steps discussed in the previous chapters, you'll have the tools you need to resolve this conflict. By now, you should understand that the driving force that keeps the conflict going is the belief that you can somehow win this fight if your determination and persistence will allow you to lose enough weight to be happy. But it can't be won, because the side that's trying to protect your autonomy is determined to fight back. Instead of trying to win, you can negotiate a durable truce that gives each side a victory.

Acceptance does not mean passive resignation to your struggle with food. Restrictive eating and unwanted overeating are both contrary to how our brains and bodies are designed. Changing that requires resolving the conflict that keeps the behavior going. It also does not mean accepting the assumed or perceived judgments of others. The ultimate source of the conflict is your own belief that you're not acceptable as you are and that you need to change. The irony is that by fighting it out on the battleground of food— restricting what you would like to eat or eating what you actually want—each side within you responds by going to the extreme, and you end up eating much more than you want.

When you stop struggling and begin accepting yourself, the two sides can get back in balance with each other. But rather than counterbalancing each other at the extreme ends, they can meet in the middle zone of moderation. When you make peace with yourself and eat no more than what you want, the urge to continue eating disappears. If you address the cause, you eliminate the effect. That's when unwanted eating can end and sustainable weight loss— without dieting—will begin.

Accepting Your Own Authority (and Uncertainty)

By now you have learned the key role that all-or-nothing thinking plays in perpetuating that conflict. In reality, life and the choices we make involve shades of gray and points on a continuum, and often you're not sure what the right choice is. This requires another type of acceptance: the ability to tolerate ambiguity and to use your best judgment, even without feeling certain that it's correct. Dieting and binge eating are both ways of avoiding this uncertainty. When you decide to diet, you follow the rules and have no further decisions to make. When you decide to binge, there are no rules, so your judgment is irrelevant.

But certainty is always an illusion. Normal eating requires recognizing the space between all and nothing. It involves making decisions without clear rules about what to do. In most areas of life, you accept the fact that you can't account for everything, so the right decision is the best choice you can make with the information available to you at the time. If you play poker, you know that you're always making decisions with incomplete information. You'll lose some hands, but if you accept that you can't know everything, you'll make better decisions with what you do know, and you'll come out ahead in the long run. The same is true in overcoming emotional eating.

Accepting uncertainty in making decisions about food will make you more willing to relinquish authority over your behavior. Recall the story about my grandparents. Grandma Gussie stepped in and took over control of Grandpa Joe's diet. Joe didn't have to stick to the rules, because Gussie was now in charge. That left him with no authority but her, and when she wasn't around, there was no one in charge. In doing this, Joe outsourced the adult role to her, which left him free to have his salty snacks when she wasn't looking.

The same surrender of authority happens when you relinquish control to a diet to tell you how to eat. The only difference is that you're just one person who's split between the two sides. The problem begins when you treat your conflicted feelings as if they're two different people. Then you separate the one who has authority, with only the power of persuasion, from the one who has signed away the adult role but still has the ultimate choice about how to behave. Most of the time, you're acting like Gussie and taking very strict charge of your diet. But when you decide to let go of that role, it's as if the side of you that's been in charge steps away, leaving the other side free to let go of control. Emotional eating is like Grandpa Joe sneaking potato chips when Gussie isn't looking.

Self-trust requires acceptance of decision-making authority

about eating, without having full confidence in your choices. But you're in charge: it's your health and your well-being, so it's your call. True, you'll make choices along the way that you may regret soon afterward, but you can learn from those mistakes, and meanwhile your body will maintain constancy. Your food intake can vary widely from day to day without any noticeable effect on your weight. Sometimes you have more of an appetite, other times less. Sometimes you're in the mood for something sweet and rich, and other times you're not. It will all even out as long as you don't go to extremes to compensate for perceived errors in judgment.

You may doubt your readiness to do this, but if you're an adult, you've been in similar situations before and you made it through. Whether it was going away to college, or beginning your first job, or moving into your own apartment, there were occasions when you questioned your readiness to take charge of your life, but did it anyway, because no one else could take over for you, so you took charge yourself.

What I'm describing here is the first thought experiment at the end of Key 4. In this scenario, an adolescent wanted to clean his room and was just about to do it, until his mother told him to. It's a scene that all emerging adults go through as they learn to be responsible for their own lives. They'll try taking charge on occasion, but will still test and challenge their parents' authority, because they want to do it on their own terms. When you accept that you're the only one in charge and take on that role in spite of not feeling prepared for it, you will, over time, become more adept and confident in your choices.

Even without clear answers to guide individual decisions, you'll know if you're making progress over time. The frequency of episodes involving emotional eating, the severity of those episodes, and, sometimes, just the simple realization that the way you think about food has changed are all good metrics for tracking progress. In fact, one of the best signs that patients I'm treating have gotten past the worst of their struggles is when they report having discovered a package of cookies in some pantry drawer or a quart of ice cream in the freezer that they had completely forgotten was in the house. They'll say, often with a sense of astonishment, "That *never* would have happened before!"

Accepting the Change Process

Signs of change such as those that I just described can say a lot. If you've had similar experiences at this point, congratulations! If not, be patient. Think realistically about where you are on whatever scale of progress works for you, and just focus on the next level. Be aware, too, that progress is not always linear. It's like Chutes and Ladders: you can move forward and then experience setbacks. The game itself began in ancient India to teach children spiritual development. It was later adopted in Victorian England as Snakes and Ladders. Instead of chutes, the players ran into moral obstacles and snakes that could set them back in their progress; but growth doesn't end there. The game teaches you to accept that there will be lapses and obstacles, but progress is measured on a larger scale.

Regardless of where you are in the process of overcoming emotional eating, or any other challenge in life, the first step is accepting the reality of where you are now. If you're at, say, level 6 on a 10-point scale of progress, acceptance means that you recognize that your starting point is 6 and your only goal for now is getting to level 7, not 10. That means recognizing and checking your mental filters, such as all-or-nothing thinking and perfectionism and using the effective coping skills you learned in Key 6, like reappraisal and problem solving.

When I began elementary school, I was among the older kids in my grade, and the principal asked my mother if she wanted me to start in first grade instead of kindergarten. Her response was, "First, let's see how he does this year, then ask me." The question never came up again, so I guess I wasn't a preschool star. But my mother was smart enough to recognize that being able to move ahead isn't the same as being ready for it, and impatience can be a setup for failure.

If you feel stuck, review the keys and exercises and think about how your filters, internal conflicts (e.g., autonomy versus belonging, "ought to" versus "want to"), and the diet mind-sets that I described may continue to affect you. But even if you've moved along in the process, you may still run into obstacles or experience setbacks. Be patient and focus on the next step, not where you were or believe you should be, but where you are.

Accepting the Urge

The last type of acceptance is to accept the urge to binge. This may seem a bit confusing, since the whole point of what you're trying to do is to stop emotional eating, which should mean not accepting it. So, to be clear, acceptance of the urge does not mean accepting the behavior that you're trying to change; it means accepting any impulse you may have to engage in it. Your instinct may be to resist even having the impulse and to try to prevent it from taking up residence in your mind, but that's not where the problem lies; the problem is acting on it, not thinking of it.

When you have an urge, the idea is already in your mind, and the more you resist it, the more it becomes firmly entrenched there. Unwanted thoughts have a way of fighting back when you attack them. But the urge itself is harmless as long as it doesn't become so fixed in your mind that you can get rid of it only by acting on it. That fixation only happens when it's resisting your effort to get rid of it, and it fights back until you're so engaged in the struggle that you've already lost it. Recall what I said in Key 2 about psychological reactance: resistance is a natural response to control. The more you try to control your thoughts, the stronger the urge will be to hold on to them.

So what should you do instead? If you've ever gone swimming in the ocean, you've probably been warned about what to do if you get caught in a riptide: never try to swim against it. Instead, the recommendation is to float or swim with the current and focus on keeping your head above water until the current has weakened and you're able to swim through it. Of course, your goal is to end up safely back on land, but the most dangerous thing you could do is to fight the current and swim directly to shore.

Those recommendations could not be more apt than when dealing with the urge to binge. Just like floating with the riptide, your thoughts about a binge are not inherently risky. They become dangerous only when your efforts to fight them create resistance that tires you out until you have no strength left to fight. So, instead of swimming against the urge to binge, float with it. Like the riptide, the urge will end before you feel the need to give in to it.

Four steps to accepting the urge to binge:

1. Notice your thoughts of wanting to binge.
2. Think to yourself: "I'm having a thought about wanting to binge."
3. Note this meta-thought: "I'm noticing that I'm having a thought about wanting to binge."
4. Think to yourself: "There is a large space between that thought and my behavior. The thought is harmless and has no power over me; I'm not compelled to act on it."

Case History: Keisha

I'll conclude with one more case history to give you a good example of how following the steps outlined in the book and accepting full authority over your food-related decisions can result in a real and lasting end to emotional eating. I'll also use it as an opportunity to review the key points mentioned in the book that this patient, Keisha, felt were most helpful to her in therapy. When she came in to see me, Keisha had been experiencing a great deal of stress and anxiety at her job. She was also binge eating every day.

Keisha grew up in a small town in the Midwest, as one of very few minority students in her school. She was an excellent student and well liked, but still felt that she had to make an extra effort to fit in. Her mother was very restrictive about her own diet and refused to allow "fun snacks" of any kind in the house. Her parents divorced while she was in elementary school, and when her mother started to work full time, Keisha moved in with her more permissive grandmother. As she put it, "For the first time in my life, I discovered a world of cookie dough and Skittles!" She made the most of that freedom while she was living there, since she didn't know how long it would last.

Keisha moved back in with her mother when she started high school, and she had gained a lot of weight during the time that she was living with her grandmother. But by the end of her first year, between her desire to fit in with her high school peers and living once again under her mother's strict diet regimen, she started to lose some of that extra weight. However, around that time she also began to struggle with episodes of binge eating, which continued through high school and college, and worsened during the three years that she had been living in Chicago before coming in to see me.

Keisha came in weekly for a total of 16 sessions. Her frequency of binge eating had already reduced significantly by the fourth session, and she was able to stop midway through the one episode that she had started that week. She said, "It was more out of habit, but I just didn't feel the need to keep on eating." The initial turning point came during the second session, when she learned how binge eating was a way to restore the balance between the need for acceptance and the need for autonomy, which struck her as a completely different way of understanding it. After the fourth week, she stopped binge eating completely, and we continued to work on ways of coping with anxiety. By the last session, she had lost almost 15 pounds without dieting and felt ready to stop coming in for weekly appointments. We agreed to meet again about two months later to follow up on her progress.

When she came in for the follow-up appointment, she had lost an additional five pounds and still had not had a single binge episode since week four. I asked her if she could tell me which of the things we discussed over the course of therapy were most helpful to her in overcoming her eating disorder. Without preparation and with very little hesitation, she was able to recite a list of the ideas that she felt had the most impact on her. I wrote them down as she responded, so I'll convey it in the order that she mentioned them, along with my best postsession recollection of her own words when she commented on each point.

Keisha's List and Commentary

Recognizing the scarcity filter

- It isn't now or never. Don't just eat because you can, and don't feel like you'll never have the chance again. Eat what you want if you want it and remember that you can always have it some other time if you don't really want it now.

Stop trying to control eating with all-or-nothing perfectionist thinking

- That kind of rigid thinking prevents flexibility, so if your eating isn't as perfect as you think it should be, instead of bending, it breaks, and you can end up bingeing. The feeling of "ought to" instead of "want to" makes it feel more controlling and like it's all or nothing.

Thinking about the Hershey's Kisses [diminishing utility] curve for mindful awareness

- Some is good, and more can be better up to a point. But then it gets worse when you overdo it, and makes the whole thing just a waste of calories. It's really about being aware of what you're doing, which makes you enjoy it more and allows you to stop eating when you're not enjoying it as much.

Understanding the balance between control and autonomy

- You need to have both, but they have to be balanced without going to the extreme of either side. If you try to balance them at the extremes, you get the worst of both worlds.

Thinking about losing weight as a natural outcome of changing how you eat

- You don't control how your body will respond to what you eat, so trying to do that or trying to make it happen faster can just boomerang and be self-defeating.

Control is about directing behavior, not restraining it

- It helps to think about it like driving a car: you can be in control of it without restraining it. It's the same with eating: you can eat less by making better choices with portions or stopping when you've had enough, instead of trying to diet. That also helps take away the need to binge, which is the best way to lose weight!

Resolving the conflict between the two sides in your head

- It's like the angel and devil on your shoulders both want you to be happy, they just have different ways of helping you do that. I think about the teenager who's about to clean his room until his mother tells him to do it. They both want the same thing, but when he feels controlled, he argues with her and doesn't want to do it anymore. Just think about what you want and do that, instead of fighting against what you think other people want you to do.

Don't overthink what to eat and trust your judgment and intuition

- This one felt hard at first, but when I got it, it was much easier than trying to think about what the right choice should be. As long as I don't overdo it and try to keep things in balance, my choice works out okay. It's the first time in my life I lost this much weight, and I wasn't even trying!

That was probably as good a summary as I could have come up with myself, but others might have a somewhat different list. After reading the book and thinking about your own eating patterns, what would you include on your list?

References

Alcott, L. M. (2016). *The complete little women.* Oxford: Benediction Classics.

American Psychiatric Association. (2013). *Diagnostic and statistical manual of mental disorders* (5th ed.). Arlington VA: Author.

Angyal, A. (1941/1967). *Foundation for a science of personality.* Cambridge MA: Harvard University Press.

Bratman, S. (2000). *Health food junkies.* New York: Broadway Books.

Brehm, J. W. (1966). *Theory of psychological reactance.* Cambridge MA: Academic Press.

Davis, C. (1928). Self-selection of diet by newly weaned infants: An experimental study. *American Journal of Diseases of Children,* 651-679.

Dostoevsky, F. (1955/2016). Winter notes on summer impressions. (K. FitzLyon, Trans.) Richmond UK: Alma Classics.

Fisher, R., & Ury, W. (2011). *Getting to yes.* New York: Penguin Books.

Freedhoff, Y. (2014). *The diet fix.* New York: Harmony Books.

Fromm, E. (1941/1994). *Escape from freedom.* New York: Henry Holt & Co.

Herman, C. P., & Polivy, J. (1980). Restrained eating. In A. Stunkard, *Obesity,* (pp. 208-225). Philadelphia: Saunders.

Kahneman, D. (2011). Thinking, fast and slow. New York: Farrar, Straus and Giroux.

Kurzban, R. (2012). *Why everyone (else) is a hypocrite: Evolution and the modular mind.* Princeton NJ: Princeton University Press.

Mann, T. (2015). *Secrets from the eating lab.* New York: HarperCollins.

Marlatt, G. A., & Witkiewitz, K. (2005). Relapse prevention for alcohol and drug problems. In G. A. Marlatt, & D. M. Donovan, *Relapse Prevention, Second Edition, Maintenance Strategies in the Treatment of Addictive Behaviors,* (pp. 1-44). New York: Guilford.

McGonigal, K. (2015). The *Upside of stress: Why stress is good for you and how to get good at it.* New York: Avery.

Ogden, J. (2010). *The psychology of eating: From healthy to disordered behavior* (Second ed.). Hoboken NJ: Wiley-Blackwell.

Pinker, S. (2009). *How the mind works.* New York: W.W. Norton.

Polivy, J., & Herman, C. P. (1985). Dieting and binging. *American Psychologist,* 193-201.

Rolls, B., & Barnett, R. A. (1999). *Volumetrics: feel full on fewer calories.* New York: Harper.

Tucker, T. (2006). *The great starvation experiment: The heroic men who starved so that millions could live.* New York: Free Press.

Wegner, D. M., Schneider, D. J., Carter, S. R., & White, T. L. (1987). Paradoxical effects of thought suppression. *Journal of Personality and Social Psychology,* 5-13.

Wilson, D. S. (2015). *Does altruism exist?* New Haven CT: Yale University Press.

Wolff, H. G. (1950). Life stress and cardiovascular disorders. *Circulation,* 1:187-203.

Yagoda, B. (2018, September). Your lying mind: The cognitive biases tricking your brain. *The Atlantic.*

Index

Note: Italicized page locators refer to figures; tables are noted with *t*.